LONESOME ROAD

Lonesome Road

A Memoir of Faith

✢

TIMOTHY P. SCHILLING

RESOURCE *Publications* · Eugene, Oregon

Resource Publications
An Imprint of Wipf and Stock Publishers
199 W. 8th Ave., Suite 3
Eugene, OR 97401

www.wipfandstock.com

PAPERBACK ISBN: 979-8-3852-1354-2
HARDCOVER ISBN: 979-8-3852-1355-9
EBOOK ISBN: 979-8-3852-1356-6

To Janke, who had not seen me before,
but has seen a lot of me since.
And to our children, Annegien and Pieter.

"Be not discouraged, keep on, there are divine things well envelop'd,
I swear to you there are divine things more beautiful than words can tell."

—WALT WHITMAN, "SONG OF THE OPEN ROAD"

Contents

Prologue

In September 2021, I reported Dad missing. He'd been off the radar before, but this time when I asked around, we realized it had been four months since anyone had seen any sign of him. The V.A. didn't know any more than we did. So I went to the police.

At that point Dad had been homeless for three years. Mom hung on for as long as she could—she'd stayed married to him for over half a century—but eventually his mind deteriorated so much she had to flee. All his meds (for anxiety, depression, PTSD, and other mental-health issues) had rendered him unable to walk, and the subsequent reduction of them left him mobile but scary. I told Mom she needed to get out of there, and finally she did—and for once, she didn't go back. But that left Dad at the house, winging it. Eventually he took off to live in an RV, and then he lost that, and then he had a car, and then he lost that. Out on the streets he'd connect with some people but freak others out. Shopkeepers said he couldn't come in anymore, and when he did they called the police. He got tossed in jail periodically, for disorderly conduct and whatnot.

And that's how I found him. It took the local police department just a day to track him down. It turned out he was in jail in his old hometown in Indiana. He'd been there sleeping in a park and was startled awake by someone walking past. Seeing the guy had a gun, Dad showed the man his knife. The guy (who had an open-carry permit) called the cops. Dad got arrested with pot and paraphernalia in his possession (illegal in Indiana) and spent two years in jail before finally facing a judge. Much of that time was spent waiting for an open spot at the state mental-health hospital so they could "restore him to competence"—to clear his head so he could stand trial for the crime he committed when it was not clear.

It did not escape my notice (my mind is sensitive to miserable irony) that the jail where Dad spent most of those two years was on the former site of the factory where his mom used to work. It's just off the road our family used to drive between our house in the country and my grandparents' house in Lafayette. Dad had been so intent on getting out of Indiana forty years before—the powers-that-be would never let him succeed there, he said—and now he'd walked voluntarily into the old trap. When I asked why he went there, he said he'd been curious.

So yeah, I found Dad. And actually, amazingly, right now, he's doing pretty well. He's got a room of his own and nice people from a local health-care facility bring him his meds, wash his clothes, and take him to the grocery store.

That's how it always seems to go. It almost pisses me off. My dad did not deserve that war or his PTSD, and our family didn't deserve their consequences. Sometimes I think I should be filing a missing-person report on Our Father in Heaven, who stands by while wars happen and families are broken, while we humans perfect our ways of killing one another. I have two children myself. I wouldn't just stand there while they tore each other apart; I'd intervene. But God lets so much happen. He looks like a worse father than I am, but surely that can't be the case. And then, just when I'm totally fed up with God, I encounter some sign of his grace and mercy—like the recent improvement in Dad's situation—that restores my faith.

This book is the story of my coming of age and coming to faith. It's about how Dad took us west and then I went east and neither of us achieved what we set out to do. It's about how failure can be a good thing.

Faith is something Dad and I have in common. I don't know anyone who loves Jesus more than he does. He told me he wouldn't have survived the war or jail without the Lord. Once, when Dad was still on the streets, I heard from someone that he showed up at the Easter Vigil. How did he even know when it was? It brings to mind the time, way back when I was kid, when I was playing with Grandma's chalkboard. After I drew a peace sign, Dad took the chalk from my hand. He drew a Chi-Rho. "This too," he said, "is a peace sign."

Battle Ground

1.

In the earliest photo in which I make an appearance, my mother stands, pregnant, in profile. Alongside her stands my father, looking down at her protruding belly. Aside from their obvious youth—they were seventeen at the time—there is nothing remarkable about the scene except my father's sweatshirt. It says, "Who cares?" That was the slogan of Dad's high school class, soon to graduate.

And an apt question it is. For in a carefree time these two young people—"seniors" only in the provisional sense of high school—had been care*less*, and now my survival was contingent upon their caring. Under the circumstances, there was no guarantee I'd be invited into this world.

I read once people are not grown up when they can care for themselves, but when they are ready to care for another. How eager were my parents to care for me?

2.

They met on a summer evening, at a drive-in called The Frozen Custard. I knew it when I was young. I can feel the receding heat and hear the crack of the bat from the ballpark across the street. I see them together. Mom calm and kind, pretty in a straightforward way. Dad fit, smart, and restless.

And so it begins. The spoon is in the custard. On a night in which you might have stayed home, you meet someone you might never have met, and this sets the course for the rest of your life.

Mom was the second of six in a Catholic family. She went to Central Catholic, their parish was St. Lawrence. Her dad worked at Alcoa. Her mom worked at a bank, when the kids got old enough to allow this. Theirs was a warm and close-knit family.

Dad's situation was different. He was the youngest of five, but often on his own. His three brothers were out the door before he started school, and his sister nearly was as well. Their dad had been a tax officer for the city. He died when Dad was twelve, of cirrhosis of the liver. After he died Dad's mom, my Grandma Mae, made meters at Duncan Electric. Dad spent his days in the park with his "buddies," a word that to me always suggested jacked-up cars and fistfights. He went to "Lafayette Jeff," the big public school. Grandma Mae was a Methodist, but I don't think Dad went to church much.

3.

It was worrisome, and embarrassing of course, when Mom got pregnant. Seeing her, Grandma asked, "When did you have your last period?"

Drawn by the warmth he felt in Mom's family, Dad took instruction and became a Catholic. He and Mom married in April. The wedding photos show him with a face full of acne. Alongside him stands his best man, his brother Gene.

Having married, the next step was to graduate, then Dad hoped to apprentice with a carpenter. That was plan anyway, but Dad upset the plan. Angling for a free day, he called in a bomb threat to school. He got the day off, but had to repeat the year. Mom graduated on time.

Three months later I was born, on August 26, 1965 in Lafayette, Indiana. A Hoosier.

Fr. Jim Bates, who'd instructed Dad, baptized me at St. Mary's Cathedral. I don't remember the baptism, of course, but words from my daughter's baptism many years later still ring in my mind: "You are a new creation, a temple of glory."

4.

Dad graduated in 1966. That apprenticeship didn't work out. He worked at Alcoa, but didn't like working in a factory, so when a recruiter came along he decided to do as his brothers had done: he would serve in the military and get the G.I. Bill to pay for college.

Years later, Mom's mom, who I just called "Grandma," said to me, "He didn't *have* to go to Vietnam. He had two children." (My sister Tracey was born a year after me.) But Dad told me he didn't think his brothers would see him as a man if he didn't serve. Gene and Bill had been in the Marines. His oldest brother, Noel, was a career officer in the Navy.

Dad joined the Army and trained at Fort Campbell, Kentucky, and Fort Polk, Louisiana. In Vietnam (from September of '67 to September of '68) he fought with the 25th Infantry Division, Charlie Company, 3rd Squadron, 4th US Cavalry. He drove an armored personnel carrier during the Tet Offensive and came home with a Combat Infantryman Badge, a Sharpshooter Badge, and a Purple Heart.

My earliest memory has him just back from the war. Wearing his green uniform, he walks in the open front door of my grandparents' home. Mom hangs up the phone, saying, "Kenny's here, I've got to go."

And go she did, and go she would. A week later we left for Fort Ord, California, the first of three times Dad would take us west.

5.

Dad never talked about Vietnam. He didn't want me playing with guns, though. One Christmas he got pissed when Grandma gave into my begging and bought me a toy machine gun.

I don't remember much from our time in California. I remember the sunshine and ocean air, and the metal stairs that led to our apartment. I remember turning out the lights when we had no candy for trick-or-treaters, and calling Grandpa when I pooped in the toilet.

Dad got his discharge in '69. He put down a plank that turned the back seat into a playpen. I like seeing us in that car, on the long drive back to Indiana. Dad had served and survived. We were heading home so our real life could begin.

6.

Muncie was, according to sociologists, a typical American town. Maybe it was. It was for me, in any case, formative. I started school there, at West View Elementary, and it was in Muncie that I first ventured out on my own. We lived on White River Boulevard, in the shadow of the dyke that kept the river from flooding our yard. A nearby hill was for me Bunker Hill. An old factory was my castle. My circle of exploration grew ever wider, though not always by choice. One morning, during the drive to school, Mom asked, "Would you like to walk home by yourself today?"

Why would I want that? I wondered.

But that's not what I said. I just said, "I guess."

She said, "Are you sure?"

That afternoon, at naptime, I felt queasy. I tried visualizing the way home, as in later years, I would imagine the ball dropping through the hoop. The first part was easy. Walk straight out the door and past the crossing guards.

Later, on the actual road, I came to an intersection, where I couldn't go straight anymore. I could only go left or right. So I stood there and cried.

A week later my uncle Greg said, "I heard you got lost."

"Where'd you hear that?" I said.

"On the radio."

But it hadn't come to that. An older girl had found me. She took me home to her mom and they called the school. As they walked me home we ran into Mom and Tracey, who were already coming to look for me.

After that I had the route down cold. But even then, it was not without risk. Once I passed a guy standing by his open garage. "Do you want some cookies?"

I said no and hurried on.

On the whole, though, I didn't feel unsafe in the world, but pretty damn at home. I worked it. I made a Dick Tracy wristwatch and secretly bought a cap-gun derringer. When big Wilson broke free on the football field, I was the only one fast enough to tackle him. In winter Tracey and I sledded the dyke and tested the ice.

School was fun too. Yes, Dick and Jane were boring, and I hated SRA readers, but once Mrs. Ellison let me pick out my own books, I was off and running. I started with a biography of Daniel Boone and never looked back.

7.

Gradually I noticed life is mysterious. A lot of things didn't make sense. Why, for example, would a crown appear on your head when you ate Imperial margarine? (It didn't, by the way.) And why did Downy have "bluing for extra whiteness," how could blue make a thing white? And why did they say M & M's "melt in your mouth, not in your hands," when any kid could see this was not true. I had colored hands every time I ate them.

And those were just the mysteries from TV. More pressing were questions like: Why does Dad stare off into space? What does he see? And why at a party would a man lie on the floor and writhe like a snake? Why would he fondle a shoe? This man was a professor. What was he a professor of?

Then there was the child on the cover of our Concert for Bangladesh album. I didn't understand how you could be fat and starving at the same time. This image related to a host of other problems I knew about, the ones Mom and Dad spoke of. Like the war, which was still going, and how Blacks and Indians got the shaft.

I wrote a poem. I called it "Why?" "Why do we fight these wars?" I asked. "Why do white people call black people the n-word?" This six-line summation—on lined paper with a crayon border—was kept in our glove box, ready for proud showings to friends and family. From what I saw, though, it did nothing to diminish the problems it addressed.

8.

I was not the only one asking questions. One day Mrs. Ellison looked over my shoulder. "Do you like hippies?"

I'd drawn a hippy in a moving van. The question brought me up short. *Did* I like hippies?

For the first time it occurred to me that my parents were hippies, and that this was visible to others. "I don't know," I said.

Mrs. Ellison moved on, but the question stayed with me. I took a quick inventory. Long hair? *Check.* Tie-dye? *Check.* Beads, incense, raggedy jeans? *Check, check, check.*

Not that Mom and Dad ever called themselves that. It wasn't like belonging to a union. They never said proudly, "We are hippies" or drank PBR on Friday at the Hippy Legion. But now that Mrs. Ellison had asked, I realized that most kids in my class did *not* have hippies for parents. When my first-grade teacher had asked us who our parents would be voting for, I'd been the only one to raise his hand for McGovern. One girl half-raised her hand.

There was in any case, I saw, a line. On one side stood my grandparents and most people in Indiana, and on the other stood my parents and some of their generation. I knew right away where I stood. I would not be a hippy.

Granted, the hippy life had its fun side. I liked water beds and bean bag chairs and coffee tables made from telephone-cable spools (the better versions of which were covered in candlewax, making a mountain racetrack for my Hot Wheels). I liked my freedom to roam and lack of a bedtime. Best of all, I liked the "Screaming Yellow Zonker," that ultimate, hippy thrill—a knotted rope of garbage bag dripping fire in the dark. This party favor, tied to a hanger and lit from below, sent flames zipping into a bucket of water. The flames made a sizzling sound when they struck, producing curls of smoke and a stench that lasted the night.

Yes, I enjoyed all of that. But there were things I didn't like, too. Like how hippies would laugh for no reason, and kill hours with their vague talk. (At parties Tracey and I were left to our own devices.) Inevitably revelers would get "the munchies," that preposterous term. (Where did everyone's brains go?) And did anyone *really* think cutoff jeans looked good, with all those loose strings hanging down? I could go on, but I'll conclude by saying that what I particularly disliked about the hippy life, was how none of the hippies I saw seemed to be getting anywhere. Later I would balk at our lack of wealth and status, but early on I was mostly irritated by the ineffective floundering that was, strangely, joined to a presumption of superiority.

I loved the hippies in my family, but I wanted *action, results.* See TV's Daniel Boone splitting the log with a single stroke. See Reed and Malloy answering the call in the night: "One Adam-12, one Adam-12, a two-eleven in progress"—the flip of the switch, the about-face of the car, the siren wailing as they proceeded to "handle code three." There was no "spacing out" here.

Nor would I do that. Examining myself in the mirror, I realized that at some point someone had stopped cutting my hair. So I got Mom to cut it.

Oh but the ambivalence! For I noted that Reed and Malloy busted people for doing what some in my own family did. Whose side was I on? One night I enlightened my sister. As a joint went around at a party, I turned to her and said, "You know, what they're doing is illegal."

Tracey said, "What's that mean?"

"Ti-im!" Mom looked at me in amazement, then she and Dad took Tracey upstairs to explain it all—how yes, it was against the law, but shouldn't be. And why was alcohol legal but pot wasn't? And the man and the system and blah blah blah . . .

Soon thereafter the universe paid me back for my mischief. Spotting a star-shaped "Police Chief" patch (in a headshop of all places), I asked Dad to buy it. To my surprise he did. When we got home Mom sewed it on one of my shirts. I wore it proudly until someone pointed out it actually said, "Peace Chief."

9.

What Mrs. Ellison didn't ask, but might've, was what my thoughts on moving were, for now we were short-timers in Muncie. My drawing of the moving van (adorned with a banner that read, "Hippy's Moving Sale") had been inspired by an actual event, the yard sale we'd held the previous Saturday. We'd cast off all that would not fit in our Ark, the gold Pontiac that would take us west. Prompting our move to Arizona was fear sparked by the killings at Kent State, and insights gained from Dad's reading of *Atlas Shrugged*. That and his admiration for the Hopi Indians.

I was fine with it. I saw myself astride the high chaparral.

And so we say goodbye to Muncie. Before leaving, though, I need to acknowledge three locals who, while just part of the scenery for me at the time, would reappear to affect the future course of my life. Two were a couple, Bob and Anita. Bob, like Dad, was an Army veteran studying at Ball State. He had a big beard and sharp sense of humor. In Muncie we saw him and Anita often, but after that we would not see them for another four years.

The other person was Fr. Jim Bates, the priest who had baptized me and instructed Dad. He now served at the Newman Center at Ball State. Our move to Muncie had kept us in touch with him. Dad liked Fr. Bates (whose look and brassy voice reminded me of Jack Benny) because he was bookish, friendly, and progressive. He'd gone to Notre Dame and Georgetown and worked as a lawyer before becoming a priest. He was only ten years older than Mom and Dad and was the one person in our life who seemed equally at home with the younger and older generation. Ironically, Grandma and Grandpa, who were older, called him "Fr. Bates," whereas Mom and Dad, who were younger, called him "Jim." Though distance would separate us, we would never quite lose touch with him.

At the end of my last day at school, Mom met me in the hall and the kids gathered round. Mrs. Ellison kissed me goodbye. To my surprise I saw tears in her eyes.

Over the years I've wondered about those I used to know. Whatever happened to them? Where did *their* lives lead? It's funny to think that many, surely, are still out there somewhere. I know you can track people down. But I don't. You can't keep it all. You have to let it go.

10.

My grandparents, of course, did not expect to find us, just a week after we left, standing on their porch. But after two nights in the state whose motto warns *Ditat Deus—God* enriches—we'd run out of money and been forced to turn back.

Mom and Dad were humiliated, but that did not register with me. I wasn't even disappointed it hadn't worked out, probably because the result was we now would live with Grandma and Grandpa, an excellent plan B.

Moreover, brief as it was, I'd gained much from our trip west. For me it was joyous. Gas stations gleamed in the desert. We drove through rainbow rocks and a forest of stone. In the mountains Tracey and I threw snowballs in the seventy-degree sun. "Up the Country" played on the radio, and "Rocky Mountain High." Whenever it got staticky I'd clamber over the seat to dial in something new. Returned to the back I stared up through the slanting rear window. On the last day the wonderful prospect had arisen of living in Jerome, a ghost town on a cliff. No, there hadn't been any jobs (just a sewing job for Mom), but our journey had been fun.

Now I shared my fried bologna with wiener-dog Sam. I loved it at Grandma and Grandpa's. Less enticing was my new school, a dank place where you pissed in a trough and the kids ate Chewy Sweet-tarts for breakfast. But that didn't matter. Our stay there was short. At summer's end we moved to a soon-to-be-beloved place, just a short drive away. There I'd put my roots as deep as I could— in Battle Ground, precious Battle Ground!

11.

Technically, we did not even live in Battle Ground. We lived out in the country, but that was the closest town, and where we went to school. We actually had West Lafayette as our mailing address, but I felt no connection to that city apart from my loyalty to Purdue.

Battle Ground, Indiana (population 806) was the site of the last major Indian battle east of the Mississippi. There William Henry Harrison's troops fought the confederacy of Indian tribes led by Tecumseh and Tenskwatawa, "the Prophet," in the 1811 Battle of Tippecanoe. The Prophet said the bullets wouldn't pierce their bodies. It didn't work out that way. The Army rebuffed the attack and razed the Indian camp, a mile away on the Wabash. That's where we lived, at riverside, on the historical site of the Indian village known as "Prophet's Town." Now that area is a state park commemorating the history, but in our time the only marker was a single metal sign.

To get to our place from Battle Ground you simply followed 225 south, turning left on the gravel-covered Huston Road, just before the river. From the road you couldn't see our house—it sat halfway down the riverbank—but clouds of dust rolled down to find us in the summertime.

Now I wonder sometimes about our stay at Grandma and Grandpa's—how that must have been for Mom, showing up broke at the tail end of misadventure. What did she say? What were the looks on my grandparents' faces? I see Mom lying awake in the back bedroom, staring at the ceiling, listening to the crickets. A car passes. A light from a car travels the walls of the room.

Three things stand out as I think back on that time. I remember the caveman suits Grandma made for Tracey and me, to wear to dress-up day at Y-camp. And the tree we stood next to when she took our picture—how small it was then compared to how big it is now. Finally, I remember the phone ringing on a sunny morning. Mom answered. She listened, and then she started to cry. She said Dad was in the hospital. He'd fallen off a pole.

12.

I didn't ask what Dad had been doing on the pole. Maybe I didn't want to know.

Through the rest of that year, Dad was in and out of hospitals. First the V.A. hospital in Indianapolis, then a local place called Wabash Valley. I didn't realize Wabash Valley was a mental hospital, didn't know what I was saying to adults when I told them he was there. I only knew what I saw: that he was depressed and couldn't work and complained about a drug called Thorazine.

But life goes on whether you understand things or not. Every morning Tracey and I climbed to the road. There was a certain grandeur to this. Through the trees we saw the bus flash yellow out on the state road. When it pulled up before us, Alice leaned over to grasp the handle. The door folded open, we ascended to her greeting.

People in Battle Ground were friendly. Not just Alice and my teachers, who would be my introduction to the communion of saints, but also Mr. Hunt, the principal, Mr. Ross, the janitor, and basically everyone else you ran into.

Tracey and I had young, pretty teachers. Tracey, in first grade now, had Mrs. Summerfeld, whose name brought to mind a field full of daisies. And I, a third-grader, was taught by Mrs. Sutter, whose sunlit, chestnut hair fell to one side as she bent to sign my free lunch card. Handing me my card, she said, "Welcome to Battle Ground."

My classmates, too, were inviting. There was Alan, fat and friendly. And Jeff, who liked to sing his Elvis Presley songs. And Lori, who danced for us one day to the Troggs' "Wild Thing" in a frumpy purple dress. Lori was a trumpet player ("like Doc Severinsen," she said). A number of my classmates lived on farms. It was fun to ride past them in the morning, as the sun burned off the frost.

Tracey made friends with the girls next door. Since no boys lived close by, I read and explored, scouring the woods for arrowheads. I found instead empty whiskey flasks and discharged shotgun shells. Mom got a job with the IRS. Dad transferred his credits from Ball State and started studying art at Purdue.

Gradually we settled into our new routine. Every Saturday Tracey and I went with Mom to do laundry at Grandma's. We burst in asking, "Grandma, do you have any fried rolls?"

"You help your mother first."

After the roll I banged on Brian's back door (he lived next door). His mom would open up: "Well hey there, Timbo!" Once Brian had downed his greasy eggs and Coke, we'd play touch football and shoot-'em-up games (Dad kindly ignored my deployment of Brian's arsenal) until Mom was ready to go. That's when Tracey and I would turn to the beloved mother of our mother to make the same request we made at this time every week: "Grandma, can we spend the night? *Please, Grandma, can we please?!*"

She'd frown, as though she hadn't seen it coming. "Spend the night?!"

Then she'd say: "Well [that Midwestern starter-word, itself a well of reflection], I [the person whose own needs are being sacrificed] guess [the mystery of this life, unfathomable and costly]."

13.

You can't do justice to people with words. Have we, here, anything more than shadows of the people I've known? Can I ever, try as I might, show them truly as they were, as they are? I could write until the end of my days, hoping to get it right, and still be nowhere near fair or adequate. But I have to try, so now a word about my grandparents.

When I think of my grandfather, I don't see a man in a hurry. In fact, in the thirteen years I knew him I saw him run only one time. That was during a family trip to Colorado, when we kids failed to bring home the younger friend we'd taken with us to a park. Seeing that, Grandpa had bolted in the direction from which we'd come. In retrospect it's a wonder he didn't have right then the heart attack that killed him later.

No, he was not one to rush. Some people have the gift of throttling down and moving slowly up the mountain. That's how he was. He took life as it came. Grandma said he had the patience of Job. On occasion I'd join him when he went to pick her up on a

Friday night from her job at the bank. That was always a busy day there, and she was often late. But he didn't mind. He just turned off the engine and sat quietly. *This, too, shall pass.*

He did stuff, of course. He worked at Alcoa. When he got home, he'd change his shoes (Grandma didn't want him tracking oil in the house) and proceed to cut the grass or rake the leaves or shovel the drive. In the summer he tended his garden, out back on their modest city lot. He grew lettuce, tomatoes, cucumbers, rhubarb, and more. He'd been raised on a farm in Benton County and still carried those fields within him. From the cucumbers he made pickles. The rhubarb we ate raw. In good weather, he cooked burgers black on the grill. As he did, I'd sidle up next to him to stare into the red coals.

Evenings were for the family. He'd pop the popcorn or join us in our game of euchre. He never got mad, never once did he speak sharply. He'd look at his cards, look out the window, look at you. Someone would make a little joke and he'd smile. Occasionally he made one himself. Years later, I'd think of him when a kid approached me at summer camp. The boy said, "I like you. You don't shout at us like the other counselors do." I figured I got that from Grandpa.

Grandma was different. Not a shouter by any means, and just as kind as Grandpa, but much more a talker and a doer. She wasn't one, like Grandpa, to just sit on the porch and watch the cars go by. She was always involved in the conversation and whatever was happening. Even in church. As soon as she got in the pew, she got right down to business, pulling out her rosary and prayer cards, reminding St. Jude of the long list of cases she had pending. Back at the house people were always dropping by to visit, but whenever they did, she would be ready for them, having already done the shopping and cleaning and baking. She knew not only whom to expect, but also what they were up to: who needed a job, whose kids were playing ball, whose mom had broken her hip. Grandma was peaceful in her own way, but more restless than Grandpa, always ready to help whatever needed helping. And she brooked no nonsense. When necessary, she read you the riot act. As she did

Grandpa one Christmas Eve—"Shame on you!"—when he'd had one too many before midnight mass. And her brother Kenny— "You jackass!—after he'd lectured the parish priest on some political matter. And then there was her boss, who she told off after he added one more task to her already endless list of duties. I won't say here exactly what she said to him—this would embarrass her, and I know she's looking down from heaven—but let me tell you, it's not what you'd expect from a pious, Catholic, Hoosier lady. In any case, the value of her willingness to call a spade a spade did not go overlooked. By the time she retired, Grandma had worked her way up from teller to vice president.

They went well together, Grandpa and Grandma. They balanced each other. God knows, they were a delight to be with. For that reason Tracey and I asked pretty much every Saturday if we could sleep over. We must've asked a hundred times before Mom told us we needed to wait first to be asked. It never occurred to me until thirty years later when I had children of my own just how much we were asking of my grandparents. Who in their right mind would want two more squabbling kids in the house, when you still didn't even have the last of your own six out the door? But Grandma and Grandpa never said no.

14.

There is a Dutch bank—I live in The Netherlands now—that used to say, "It starts with ambition." This was before the bank was taken over, divided up, and needed a government bailout to survive. But I like the slogan (I'm a sucker for a good ad campaign), and it seems true to me, since the "it" is unspecified. Whatever we become stands in relation to some prior conception that gets the ball rolling. Even if we don't become what we envision, the place where we end up reflects where we set out for.

My own plan was simple and beautiful. In the year 2000 I would be, at age 35, elected the first President of the new millennium and the youngest President ever. This idea arose from a little math calculation and from biographies I checked out from the library. I read any I could get my hands on, and many were of the

Presidents. By nine I'd shelved notions of becoming a spy or detective in favor of becoming commander in chief.

Beyond ambition, I had fiery resolve. I was getting A's and I would get A's. That was how you made it, everyone said, by applying yourself. By going for it. By doubling down and sticking to it. The books showed not only the destination, but how to get there. How did FDR and JFK do it? Simple: by going to Harvard, then to law school, and then running for office. A-B-C.

Fortunately, I didn't have to work hard to get the grades. The times table came easily and our lack of a TV encouraged my reading. I loved school. My teachers were great, and school was where the kids were. So I racked up stars on the reading chart, whipped my fellows at multiplication baseball, and responded eagerly when I was assigned extra work. After I wrote a story about a man falling into the fourth dimension (a place I'd read of in a comic book), Mrs. Sutter wrote "Superboy!" on my report card. That word was even better than the free meal my A's got me at McDonald's. I treasured that word. I buried it deep in my heart.

15.

"What do you think?"

"About what?"

"Well, what do you think?"

I hated that question. I never knew why Dad asked it. It made me squirm. I gathered he was just making conversation, but with me it never worked. Worse was when he asked whether I liked a piece of art he'd made. Like the thousand nails he'd pounded into a plank. Some of the nails were bigger than others, some were rusty, and the nails were driven to various depths. It looked like the surface of the ocean.

"How do you like it?"

"I like it." Which is what I always said, just to get it over with. Usually I didn't get what Dad was up to, but I didn't want to hurt his feelings. I thought art should be something nice looking that made sense, not smeared paint or a ripped shirt hanging on the wall.

But I wasn't lying when I said I liked it. I *did* like it, because he'd made it and I loved him and I could see it was important to him.

More troubling than such exchanges was what an art degree would do for him and for us. I knew kids whose dads were farmers or construction workers, and one who bragged his dad was a truck driver, but I didn't know any artists. Dad said his favorite, Van Gogh, had never made a dime. Meanwhile, on Mom's salary, we were just scraping by. We drank powdered milk instead of regular milk and picked up free commodities (cheese and apple juice) from a government warehouse. At home we hardly had any furniture, so Tracey and I slept on mattresses on the floor. Having spotted cockroaches, I spent the first night there bolt upright with a can of Raid. Some weeks later I found a dead mouse in my sheets. Mom and Dad solved that problem right away—bought some wood and Dad built us beds—but they couldn't keep the winter wind out of our house with no insulation. We had to open the oven door and wear blankets to keep warm.

These things I kept to myself. I didn't need to have kids in the house. Harder, though, was knowing what to do with the question, "What does your dad do?" Adults often asked this when they first met you. Saying Dad was going to Purdue was borderline acceptable (Shouldn't he be done with that by now?), but saying he was studying art yielded puzzled, noncommittal nods.

Conceivably, a solution was offered by my fourth grade teacher, Mrs. Brown. (Mrs. Brown! A grandmother to us all. Round and soft like Grandma Mae.) The school, she said, was looking for an art teacher: "Would your dad be interested?"

I said I'd ask. But I was deeply grateful when Dad showed no interest. For much as I wanted him to have a job, I did not want him on my turf, with his long hair and scraggly beard, going on about something none of us understood.

16.

Though times were tough, the way life *should* be was visible and within reach. When you left our road for the state road, the first place you passed on the right was a white farmhouse on a vast expanse of lawn. That's where Kathy lived, a pretty girl in my class who played the flute. Kathy was my main competition for top grades. I must say, though, I never had the sense she was competing. There was no fever about her. To this day I imagine her playing her flute in a glade, for birds who've stopped to listen.

Behind Kathy's house stood a barn and greenhouse, a research site of Purdue University. Kathy's dad was a research agronomist, which means a farmer with brains and status to boot. Their neat yard contrasted with our jumble of rocks and weeds, where one day we found our landlord (who sold cuckoo clocks) swimming nude! The difference between my world and Kathy's was summed up one morning on the bus. Kathy was about to board, but realized she'd forgotten her lunch. As she ran to get it, her mom held the door. The boy next to me leaned to look inside. "They're watching *The Today Show*," he reported. "At my house we watch cartoons."

I turned back to my book, *Charlie and the Chocolate Factory*. Poor Charlie! At least my grandparents had their own homes and beds. But Charlie and I were alike in our dream. Out there, somewhere, lay the golden ticket. I was grateful to Charlie, for when I entered into his troubles I could forget my own, and feel understood at the same time. This reprieve was especially welcome in the winter. When the roads were bad, Alice would be late and it would take the whole 40-minute ride to get your toes unthawed. I never rode that bus without a book.

17.

Joining me in tribulation was my sister Tracey. Up to a point we were similar. We looked alike (with the same nose and freckles) and Tracey, too, was a quick study. To my consternation, they even talked about skipping her a grade. (Did that mean she was smarter than me?)

But she had a hotter temper than I did, tipping the Monopoly board when I pissed her off, and she made choices I wouldn't make. Like when a boy came selling candy bars. Tracey had just gotten money for her birthday so she bought the whole box. No, that wasn't me, to impulsively buy the box.

Another way were different was in our response to Dad. She always seemed more troubled by his melancholy, as though she felt his pain more deeply. I saw it on her face. Then again, she clashed with him more too. If she disagreed, she'd let him know. I didn't have the stomach for arguments with Dad. No good came of it. I didn't mean to dwell on his troubles or wrangle with him any more than I had to. I had better things to do.

18.

Dad never did get that B.A. The specifics elude me. What I remember is the pattern that repeated itself: the new plan followed by conflict, disillusionment, and another change of direction. After Purdue, Dad worked as a groundskeeper. Whenever he had a job we were delighted. It brought an infusion of cash and well-being. We hurried to reduce our deficit, buying first the TV that allowed me to join in the schoolyard chorus of approval after every showing of *Happy Days*. Having a TV also gave me new players to be when Brian and I played football. Since I'd seen very few games, the only player I normally could think to be was Jim Thorpe, the Indian star from Carlisle who'd been stripped of his Olympic medals for having played semi-pro baseball. I'd read his biography upon Dad's recommendation. I doubt Brian, who was usually Dick Butkus, even knew who Thorpe was. Dad, for that matter, got me to read about other people too: like Mahatma Gandhi and Martin Luther King.

Yes, our dreams expanded when Dad had a job. Maybe we'd get a new car, maybe even an Audi. During these times I hoped someone would ask me what my dad did. *Go ahead, ask me.*

But inevitably something happened. Dad had a tough time with bosses. Or they had a tough time with him. He'd quit or get fired. He and Mom hashed it over at dinner. "The guy's a bastard—you can't work for someone like that."

Tracey and I cleared the dishes. Dad grabbed a beer. The conversation flagged, then flared again: "Where was he during the war?" I washed and Tracey dried, the water getting colder and greasier. When the last pan was put away we left Mom and Dad to their tears and sinking candle, the dismay petering out finally in exhaustion.

19.

People were not oblivious to our need. When our car broke down—always only a matter of time—Grandma and Grandpa paid for the repair, though Mom hated to ask. Another benefactor was Uncle Gene. One Sunday he showed up with binoculars and a *Childcraft* encyclopedia. The binoculars were ideal for scanning the opposite riverbank, and the encyclopedia was even better, with its fine drawings and cache of historical stories. When Gene learned I collected stamps and coins (Grandma kept her eye out for good ones at the bank), he offered to take me along on one of his sales trips. A shop along the way sold coins. On the appointed day he brought along a pillow to raise me up in the car, that I might better see out. I acquired some wonderful treasures: Indian-head pennies, a Buffalo nickel, a Liberty dollar . . .

Fr. Bates came to see us as well. Tracey and I tagged along while Dad showed him the river. Fr. Bates needed to tread carefully in his shiny black shoes, especially on the log that led down to the lowest level. While Dad talked, our priest friend listened, turning occasionally to ask Tracey and me about school and our interests. His clangy laughter reminded me of old relatives, fishing boats, and the Cubs on WGN.

Afterwards Dad would raise again with Mom the prospect of going to church, a practice that had fallen by the wayside. "Jesus is Lord," he said. But Mom was not interested, for which I was grateful. From my occasional church attendance with Grandma and Grandpa, I knew it to be a twilight zone of strange rituals, contrived language, and blue-and-white bleeding statues. Not for me!

20.

When you're young your struggles seem big and unique and the only ones that matter. But they're not, of course. Slowly my eyes got opened. As when a boy at school told us his mom had been busted for growing pot. "She didn't even know it was there," he said. Yeah, right. Then a girl on the bus said her dad had lost his job and times were so hard she had to eat "toast for a snack." Well, I ate toast for a snack all the time!

Nonetheless, though I felt deprived, I later realized that almost no one in Battle Ground was well-to-do. And of what did my poverty consist? A lack of brand-name snacks? By the standards of the world I was rich indeed. I never went hungry. Our basic needs were met. My sweet and dutiful mother worked hard at her job and at home to keep us clothed, fed, and off welfare. But you don't understand that when you're a kid comparing his life to the perfections of *Happy Days*.

What I did know was that some kids had it harder than me. Those were the ones with problems they couldn't hide. One girl who rode our bus, for example, was seriously obese. When she was late, she'd come running out of her trailer, her flesh jiggling. You didn't want to see that. When I did, my heart went white with sadness. Once she slipped in class, during a spelling bee. The sound of her flab smacking the tile brought an explosion of laughter.

And then there was that laughter another time, with another girl. Mrs. Sutter brought her in one morning, a new girl. Right away I saw there was something unusual about her. It was her eye. What was up with that eye? It was very big and cloudy blue.

Mrs. Sutter brought her to the table Alan and I shared. To two nice boys, boys she could trust. I sensed Alan was looking at me, but I was not by any means going to look at him. I kept focused on my pencil instead. Maybe I could go sharpen it. Maybe I could keep focused on the as-yet-unsolved sums on my ditto. Then Alan whispered, "She has a horse's eye."

Well, that did it. It was as if he'd slit open a bag of marbles. Our giggles went everywhere.

Welcome to Battle Ground.

21.

But you don't go to those girls. You don't ask later how they're doing, or open up or befriend them. Instead you scramble all the harder so as not to sink in your own muck. Maybe that's why I never swam in the river or the tiny pond in our yard: because that brown water and sucking mud reminded me too much of the swamp within myself. (Of that and the rats that ran in our walls.)

Maybe that's why I took to basketball, because it was clean and out in the open and upwardly directed. I played every day at recess, with Brent and Roger. I loved the well-defined target, and rewarding swish. One day our teacher, Dr. Bryan, (we were in fifth grade now) said: "You boys should join the team."

Practice was at noon on Saturday, but I was ready by seven. I kicked the ball out of bounds on my very first fast break, but I soon got the hang of it. I played whenever I could. Enjoying basketball was the most natural thing in the world in Indiana, land of "Hoosier hysteria." But it worked for me, too, because it was a game I could practice on my own. Playing catch required a partner, but shooting hoops I could do by myself. Seeing my devotion, Mom and Dad got me a basket for my birthday. Dad attached it to a tree by the road. There in the dirt (dodging the roots) I developed my jump shot: starting in close at first, making sure I had the technique down.

At the library I found a book on Bill Bradley, who'd been an All-American at Princeton and then a Rhodes scholar. That sounded right. The A's were already coming, now I just needed to up my game-game!

22.

Shooting hoops, like reading books, offered refuge as tensions rose steadily at home. Dad was ever more tightly wound, and the bottle didn't help. He kept running into the same obstacles. His long hair made it hard to find a job, but he sure wasn't going to cut it. (His brothers had gotten on him about this as soon as he'd gotten out of the Army.) Another obstacle was his spotty work history and lack of a degree. So we might get excited about job listings—"They're hiring bus drivers for four dollars an hour!"—but that didn't mean Dad was going to get or keep one.

An obstacle, too, was Dad's way of communicating. He did not speak as most men did. A lot of men barely spoke at all, they just watched the game. But Dad tended to go on about the rot in the system, the misery of the underclass, and the conspiracies that led to our wars. He was for "the little man," and it took little to get him started. Maybe you had no such intention of that, maybe you were just making some Kool-Aid when he'd spotted you. "Get this," he'd say, the "this" being followed by a series of reflections you would never have dreamed could arise from so humble a word. "Yeah," I'd say, "interesting," or "I never thought of it that way," which had the unintended effect of leaving the door open to elaboration. Gladly walking through it, he probed the fault lines in society and within the human person, his conclusion being— among others—that you need to stand up for what's right (as Jesus did), but you also need to know how to defend yourself. To which end he explained how to disable a man without using a weapon (by stomping the knee, punching the throat, driving the nose bone up into the brain).

No, there were quieter, more subservient men for bosses to hire. After the latest rejection Dad would open a beer while Mom fried potatoes and assured him things would turn around.

"Why do you even stay with me?"

"What do you mean," she said, "why do you say that? Because you're *kind*. You're *faithful*. You speak the truth and try to do the right thing. It's not your fault the world is so screwed up."

"I suppose."

"I know we're tight for money, but you do what you can. Look at that couch you made. It's great. Don't quit on us. Don't give up."

Dad had made the couch from Great Aunt Blanche's barn wood. We'd gotten the wood for free at the estate sale. The couch was nice, I had to admit, though I preferred store-bought.

Dad thought it over. "Maybe. But you would have been better off with someone else." And here the conversation took its little turn. (How many times have I done this myself? *Don't go there*, I think. *Don't say it. It's not fair. You know where it will lead.* But then I've done it anyway. Said the one word. Poked at the weak spot.) "Like how about with" Dad said, invoking the name of the high school friend of Mom's who'd visited us once in Muncie. He'd given Dad LSD and led him down a rat hole of a trip.

Dad hated his guts.

Now I never saw Mom show any interest in this guy whatsoever, and after that night he was never seen again. But Mom had to defend herself time and again.

"You don't love me. Why would you?"

23.

What's worse, the scurrying in the walls or the scurrying in your mind? At first we didn't see the rats, we just heard them. Then we trapped one behind the fridge. I don't know how we got rid of it, I don't want to know. The next day our landlord brought poison and when we came home we found ten in the living room. One tumbled down the stairs, as if it were drunk. We turned right around and went to Grandma and Grandpa's. The landlord cleaned them up. After that we didn't have a rat problem anymore. I guess the smell of their dead brothers scared them away.

24.

Life went up and down. Saturday was a day of pleasure. I asked Grandpa if I could make some money. He put his hands on his hips, looked around, grabbed some clippers. "Why don't you clip the weeds off the back fence?" I spent the money on comic books and Lik-M-Aid. Then I ran laps around the cemetery with my aunt Mary. She was on the track team. After dinner we watched CBS's killer lineup: *All in the Family, Mary Tyler Moore, Bob Newhart, Carol Burnett*. Fun!

But then came Sunday. Just church (on the rare occasions when I accepted Grandma's invitation), old movies on WGN, and homework. The family dinner at one o'clock was never fun food, like pizza or hamburgers, but a roast and mashed potatoes and vegetables and rolls—as if we were all still living on the farm. Mom and Dad's arrival, shortly before it started, put me on alert. Who knew what Dad might say?

One Sunday they were late. At first I was glad. The delay meant I had more time to play with Brian. But by three the sky had turned a sickly yellow—sign of an imminent thunder shower. It matched the unease in my belly.

Mom and Dad showed up right before it rained. On the way home we heard all about it. About the narc who'd followed them from the concert, and the arrest, and the night in jail. That's when I learned what a bail bondsman is.

Later we all laughed about the cop who couldn't identify the people he'd arrested. The charges were dropped. But laughter was the exception, worry was the rule.

25.

That was the summer of the Bicentennial. We'd spent months getting ready for it, studying not only the revolution, but our local history as well: George Rogers Clark, Fort Ouiatenon, pioneer ways. We dressed in old-timey clothes and spun thread and pulled taffy. But then it was over. After the ships and fireworks people were done with history. It was all just the present again.

Dr. Bryan came to take me to the free basketball camp at Harrison High. He picked up all of us who didn't have a ride. That was a fine time, us piled in the back of his truck, catching the breeze. It was nice of him, we agreed. This was his vacation after all.

Dr. Bryan was my fourth great teacher in a row, after Mrs. Ellison in Muncie, and then Mrs. Sutter and Mrs. Brown in Battle Ground. He'd gotten his Ph.D. in education, so he was very committed to his work, and as a teacher he saw the individual. If you got ahead in your assignments, for example, he'd let you disassemble a lawn mower. (It was easier to take apart than put together). When I was trying to earn the President's Physical Fitness Award, he stood by patiently during his lunch break while I practiced pull-ups.

Tracey was around, too, of course, but increasingly I could see we were going our separate ways (when we weren't huddled together worried about Mom and Dad). I saw it in the books she read. They were always about kids with problems. Not nice clean problems, like Teddy Roosevelt being weak and made fun of for wearing glasses, but then learning how to box and fire a rifle and going on to become President. No, her books featured the problems you saw on the ABC after-school specials, like divorce and drug abuse. Messy, close-to-home stuff that I didn't want to think about.

Granted, I did have my own secret fascination with misery. Stevie Wonder's "Living for the City," often on the radio, gave me the willies, as did David Wolf's biography of Connie Hawkins, *Foul!*. Hawkins of Bed-Stuy! "Long Tall Sally," taking his calls at the pay-phone and running around in flappy shoes. I knew it was absurd to compare my situation to Hawkins's, but somehow I could totally relate.

But what do you do with your gloom? Do you stay in it or do you crush it and move on? I was of the latter camp. FDR didn't sit around and brood and sink into the Depression, he bit down on his cigarette holder and fired up the machinery of government. He fixed the economy and won the war. Tracey, however, seemed to have no plan to rise above it. She seemed more drawn to the chaos of the world at hand. Seeing *Go Ask Alice* lying on her bed—Tracey was ten at the time—I picked it up. I'd heard about it. It was about a girl dealing with sex and drugs. Curious, I started reading. I must admit, it did grab you. But halfway through, I tossed it aside. Alice was so stupid! She was going down, but I wasn't going with her.

26.

Four years before—on December 23, 1972, to be exact—Dad had lifted me up and set me down on the counter in our kitchen. We were about to make the two-hour drive from Muncie to Lafayette, where we would spend Christmas with my grandparents. "When we get there," he said, "we'll go skating and drink hot chocolate. Tomorrow we'll go to midnight mass, and on Christmas morning we'll open presents." In my mind I saw the colored lights and the presents, and in my father's eyes I saw the delight he took in telling me these things. This was how it was supposed to be. That was what he wanted. Don't we all? Aren't we born wanting those things?

So why then does life go as it goes? Why does rightful hope get bushwhacked and turned into its opposite? Why must I give you that same hopeful father losing it on a summer evening after half a bottle of tequila?

The evening began as any other, but in the delicate machinery that was our life, a gear slipped or a hinge broke. The structure finally gave. I heard my parents' voices rise. Dad was furious. He shattered a glass. It was over, he said. He was leaving, for Florida. Why Florida, I couldn't imagine. Then Tracey said the thing that stunned me: "I want to go with Dad."

I couldn't believe it. How could she even consider it? I pictured her clinging to him on the back of a motorcycle. Not long before, we'd all been with him as he'd driven angry and drunk on the back roads. We'd shouted, "Stop, Dad, stop!"

Now Mom said, "No, Tracey, you're not. Kids, let's go."

"Where are you going?" he said.

"I don't know, but I've had enough."

"Well then," he said, "I guess we won't be needing this." And with that he launched himself at the couch he'd made, demonstrating perfectly the karate kick I'd once tried to describe in a story.

The slats separated from the back, the top from the bottom.

We raced to the steps that led to the road, but Dad, quick as he was, jumped ahead of us. He loomed above us in the electric light, a hulking shadow blocking the way.

He raised his hand to strike. "Where are you going?"

Mom just looked at him.

He dropped his hand and let us go.

27.

I thought we were going to Grandma and Grandpa's, but Mom stopped at a payphone and called Grandma Mae.

Grandma Mae was a very sweet lady. She was short and kept her hair piled in a bun. She ran the cage-style elevator at the courthouse. She wore cat-eye glasses and called me "Sugar" and "Dear heart." We didn't see her as often as Grandma and Grandpa. She lived in a small apartment. One time she'd come out to the river to cook us ham with pineapple.

She let us in and made room on the couch. She clasped my hand between her two. As Mom told the story she blinked slowly and then brought her fingers together at her lips. "Oh Kay, I am so sorry."

Grandma Mae took the couch and Tracey and I slept with Mom in the one bed. In the morning we went to Grandma and Grandpa's. There I sat in the living room as Mom discussed it with Grandma. The radio was turned to WASK. At home we listened to WAZY. I heard Grandma say, "Do you want me to call a lawyer?"

28.

That Saturday Mom drove us home. Dad apologized, then Mom and Dad told us they were separating. We cried. They sent us out so they could talk.

We sat up by the road. I doodled with a stick.

An hour later Mom called us down. She said they were going to give it another try.

After that, some things got better and some things got worse. What got better was Dad quit drinking and Mom and Dad stopped fighting. Tranquility returned to our home.

What got worse was their relationship with Grandma and Grandpa. At some point Grandma said something Mom didn't like. Mom felt she had to choose.

She chose Dad. We started doing our laundry at a laundromat on the West Side. Tracey and I went to Grandma and Grandpa's less often. When we did, Mom dropped us off without saying hello.

29.

Oddly enough—in the strange way of life—everything else for me suddenly turned golden.

I won the school spelling bee and then won the county final. Mr. Hunt called an assembly and gave me a plaque. A reporter came to interview me and I got my picture in the paper. He asked, "What was the hardest word?"

At basketball I got better and better. Every day I biked to the schoolyard to work on my moves. I mastered the reverse layup and hook shot. Inspired by my fevered play-by-play, I pulled off miraculous upsets, bringing Battle Ground back from sixteen down. (*How does he do it, folks, double-teamed and injured? Still, the Tomahawks are going to need a miracle to pull this one off.*) How I hit those game-winners, from thirty feet out with me falling out of bounds, I'm still not sure.

Now I was in junior high, a seventh-grader. I'd left the familiar elementary school for the stately, three-story, brick building that had once been a high school. It had polished wooden floors and a trophy case from the glory days that I presumed soon would return.

On the first day of school, our class advisor called us together. "We need a class president. Who wants to run?"

I alone raised my hand. Then every other hand rose to elect me.

30.

The most delicious development, however, was still to come. The seed had been planted earlier that year. Many times from the bus I'd admired a hoop and paved court just up the road. Two girls from our school lived alongside it. When I played at our place, my ball got dirty, but this looked ideal. "Come on," I said to Tracey. Let's go for a walk. Maybe they'll be out."

Happily, they were. We said hi as we walked past—then deliberated, as though the idea had just come to us.

"Would you mind if we joined you?"

They didn't.

Cindy was an eighth-grader. She was the star of her team. She had curly hair and a ready smile. After that I often went back there, but always alone. Cindy was the only girl her age with a jump shot.

We'd both seen *One on One*. "Wasn't that great?" she said.

When Cindy's girlfriend wrote Cindy's and my initials in a heart in condensation on a window of the bus, I let it stay.

"Do you like her?" she asked.

Cindy and her friends started eating lunch with me and mine.

How could something so simple as holding hands flip your heart the way it did?

We went roller skating. "Puppy Love" played, and "You Light Up My Life." They were awful but, under the circumstances, not too bad.

31.

This was when Bob and Anita re-entered our life. They lived in Seattle now. It was fun to have visitors, we didn't have many.

"You'd love the Northwest," they said. "It's so beautiful."

Dad decided to check it out. He left on the Greyhound.

When he called, I said, "I suppose you've heard I've been holding hands."

I dreaded what he'd find there.

32.

He returned just before Thanksgiving, in time to see my first game. I scored six of our first eight points, including a driving layup off the opening tip-off. Cindy watched as well.

That night in bed I thanked God for all that was good in my life.

Dad said the weather was much milder in Seattle. "And there's a job waiting. He can take me on as a roofer."

Through the window I saw our empty doghouse and undriveable driveway, the cut that led from the road to the river.

33.

Cindy's mom said she'd gone into town. I stuffed my ball in my pack, biked the grainy pavement, accelerated to climb the slope. At the railroad tracks I paused to consider. I'd always liked this spot, where the roads converged. From here you could see the water tower, the post office, the little grocery.

Where was her bike? Where could she be?

The yards were all empty.

I went to the playground and worked on my hook shot. But my heart wasn't in it.

A man raked leaves into a burning pile. He had Purdue on the radio. Mark Hermann was the quarterback then. The wind picked up. A leaf fell trustingly into the flames.

34.

Mom said, "You'd better call Cindy and let her know. You don't want her crying at school."

I'd never called her before. My belly shrunk to a buckeye.

At least I could say Dad had a job out there. This wasn't just some half-baked plan of people totally adrift in this world.

I looked at Grandma, my partner in euchre. She had blue veins on the back of her hands. "Pick it up," she said.

35.

That December our lamp gave off smoke instead of light. Dylan's "Desire" unspooled repeatedly on the tape deck: *Joe-ey, Joe-ey!* Why did we always have to listen to this? I hated his melancholy droning—his absurd clothes and fur-trapper hat. What was he so depressed about? He was a multimillionaire rock star!

On my last day the kids gave Cindy and me the back seat. But we'd never kissed and wouldn't now, not with me warding off tears.

Grandma and Grandpa gave us our gifts early. I got a green warm-up suit for basketball. I don't know what Tracey got.

At the beep of the horn, we went to the porch. Mom and Dad sat in the car, trying not to look. Grandpa and Grandma hugged us. Then we took our gifts and crossed the sorrowful separation.

Port of Angels

1.

"I'm thinking of breaking up with Katie."

"What? Why?" Wyatt looked truly surprised.

"I don't know. She's in Victoria now. I've still got this whole year ahead of me. I just feel so restless. This is holding me back. I'm missing out." I let him out in front of his house.

"Well, yeah, then you should do it."

I mean, there were a lot of hot girls, and I had a lot of capital. What was I supposed to do, just waste it? So I did it. I ended it. Katie and I were watching *Fail-Safe* on TV, a film I'd watched in Contemporary Issues. I stayed tight-lipped, focused on the film. Then we made out and afterwards I got quiet and she said, "What's wrong?"

I said it wasn't working for me anymore, and she said, "Well why'd we just do that then?" And I said, "That's when I knew."

But I guess I'd already known before.

You wonder sometimes what you want. Katie was bright, an athlete, a cheerleader. She was good looking and easy to be with. People loved her. Ten months before it had started perfectly, with snow and a moonlit walk down the railroad track. But then she graduated and left to study in Canada. Now when she arrived on the ferry for a visit it took me an hour to get used to her again. Suddenly my freedom was gone. And at school we had all these other girls, fresh-faced beauties at the football games and student council meetings. Me rapping my gavel.

Three years before, on my first day at P.A. High, I'd noted the pecking order. Sitting opposite us at the registration table were the smiling cheerleaders ("Are you comin' to the game? You *gotta* go to the game!") and at the end of it stood Hoine, the student body president, a big blond ballplayer.

Now I was the guy. And I was going to savor it. This was going to be quite a year. I started keeping a journal. I gave every day one-to-five stars.

2.

But damn, it had taken some doing getting there! The dude at the back, freshman year, eyeing my book bag and grinning: "Hey man, waddaya got in there, a typewriter?" And me grinning back to keep on his good side (for he was known to pound on guys). Ignoring, too, the teasing whisper of a girl who pretended to like me ("Isn't he cute?"), as her laughter trailed across the room. Just when I was getting the hang of Seattle (sort of), we'd moved to Port Angeles, where a classmate took one look and bluntly informed me: "Short hair is out." My khakis were a problem as well. I was the only kid in the school who didn't wear jeans every day. So I fixed it: let my hair grow, got a job bagging groceries, bought myself some jeans. Most importantly, I signed up for "intensified" classes that put me in a safe cocoon of mild-mannered strivers.

Over time I surprised even myself with my knack for seizing the opportunity. At the end of my sophomore year I'd caught potential rivals sleeping and run for junior class president unopposed. That positioned me well for the run, a year later, for student body president. That, too, looked to be a done deal, until I heard that Heckman had Vick on board as his running mate. I hadn't been worried about Heckman—he'd pissed too many people off over the years—but Vick was a clone of Hoine, a big, popular, easygoing jock. Hell, *I'd* vote for Vick. So I went to Vick. We were friendly enough from basketball. I said, "This is really important to me. I'm asking you not to run." I said if I won I'd appoint him student court judge. And so it went. I don't even know why he did it. Maybe it was nothing more than an act of simple human kindness. Must've fired up Heckman, though.

Yeah, I was relentless in those days. On election day Vice-President Amy was worried—"I don't know, I just don't know if we're going to pull this off"—and I said, "Quit wasting time. We need to drag people to the polls!" I even got Vick to do it. Corralled him in the hall, pulled him over to introduce him to some impressionable underclassmen. "Tim," I said (for his name was Tim, too), "why don't you escort these lovely ladies to the voting booth?"

Yes, working it!

3.

Port Angeles, Washington is in the northwest corner of the lower forty-eight states. When we moved there I figured we were done moving west. If we went any further, we'd fall off the map altogether. A small city (of 17,000 when we arrived), Port Angeles sits on the northern shore of the Olympic Peninsula, just across the water from Canada's Vancouver Island. We used to see the Olympic mountains that back Port Angeles from our window in Seattle. Now we lived in their shadow. Originally the place was named for Mary, the Mother of God. In the eighteenth century the Spanish had sailed up the Strait of Juan de Fuca, dropped anchor, planted a cross, and claimed it for Christ and King. They called the harbor formed by the natural sandspit *Puerto de Nuestra Señora de los Ángeles*: Port of Our Lady of the Angels.

We came because we'd needed to get out of Seattle. Seattle! "The Emerald City," they were calling it now. Doomed from the start. We hadn't even gotten out of Indiana before the trouble began. *Is that smoke?* No, it was steam. Dad pulled over near Crawfordsville and had me help him move boards from the U-Haul to the back of our station wagon. That balanced the load and kept the car from overheating. But that trailer was simply too big. Days later, driving in moonlight in the Rockies, Mom hit some ice and the trailer started fishtailing, swinging us between the wall of rock on the left and thousand-foot plunge on the right. Dad grabbed the wheel and somehow pulled the trailer back in line.

Seattle itself seemed fine at first. We lived on Beacon Hill, one of Seattle's seven hills ("like Rome!"), and our bungalow was much nicer than the house we'd had on the river. It had wooden floors, a big plate-glass window, and a washing machine in the basement. Unlike in Indiana, the yards in our neighborhood were not flat but sloping, and they had typically not a lawn of grass, but a Japanese-style mix of rocks and cedar bark surrounding the ferns and fir trees. On the first day in our new house, January 1, 1978, Warren Moon led the Washington Huskies past Michigan in the Rose Bowl. Purdue never beat Michigan. Maybe it was a sign. And Dad did have a job, for a while. Mom too, of course (she always did), having gotten on with the Social Security Administration. But then Bob and Anita split up, soon after we arrived. And our car broke down, which meant Dad had no way to get to work. And he hated it anyway, because the tight crawl spaces reminded him of tunnels in Vietnam. Then we discovered there was a lot of crime in the neighborhood. The corner grocery got robbed, and I got robbed, while collecting on my paper route.

Summing up the badness was a night when Mom and Dad heard a cry for help. They thought it was a domestic dispute, but then realized the cry came from a car parked right in front of our house. Dad opened the trunk with a crowbar. Locked inside were a woman and her son. Two men had accosted them as they pulled into their garage. They'd raped the woman and put mother and son in the back and driven it until they realized they couldn't drive a stick (the woman could hear them grinding the gears). Eventually they had abandoned the car. Freed from the trunk, the woman and boy came into our house. He was a year or two younger than me. We stood awkwardly, waiting for the police to arrive. I apologized for our lack of furniture. I lied, saying it hadn't arrived yet. "That must be tough," he said.

The crime on Beacon Hill made me afraid to sleep at night. I liked summer because the days were longer, but darkness always came eventually. Sadly, school offered no respite either. I'd thought I'd make a splash, but Mercer Junior High was overwhelming, with 1300 students and a lot of racial tension. I adapted. I avoided risky situations. By eighth grade 1 was feeling reasonably at ease and probably would have been fine staying, but then Tracey faced trouble that made the point moot. Some boys started hassling her at school. Maybe they liked her, maybe they just resented her smarts. In any case, she was never one to back down. In Battle Ground she'd punched a boy for giving her grief. Now a boy had tried to get in her pants. She'd fought him off, but later that day had run away with one of her friends. The girls were gone for two days before the police found them, at the mall in Everett.

4.

That did it. Dad called Uncle Gene: could he loan us some money? We withdrew from school, never said goodbye to anyone. Grandma and Uncle Gene offered to take us in for the summer while Mom and Dad looked for a new home. Grandma got us plane tickets.

It was good to be back in Indiana. But even in that short time much had changed. I had, for one. I was both more worldly (I'd gone west and lived in a big city) and chastened (for I'd struggled and accomplished seemingly little). Battle Ground, too, had changed. I arrived in time for the last day of school and joined my old classmates as they moved desks from the soon-to-be-demolished junior high. A new school had been built on the edge of town. I saw Cindy holding hands with the boy who had taken my place.

The biggest change, though, was that Grandpa had died. He'd had a heart attack in church earlier that year. The doctor said his heart had been damaged by smoking and stress. Mom believed Grandpa, like Dad, had a war-troubled mind. He'd been a Navy medic at Iwo Jima and had been sent home after he'd been shot. Grandma gave me his Purple Heart. I felt bad knowing Tracey and I must have worn him out with our fighting. I missed him.

Gene and Aunt Margaret were kind to us. Every weekday morning, before Grandma went to work, she drove us out to their ranch house and acres of lawn. They had a piano, a pool table, and HBO in the game room. They got us a membership at the Y and took us to see "Annie" on stage in Chicago. When I wanted to make money, Gene had me cut the grass on his riding mower. One Friday he got me thinking about college as we washed his car. "You're grades are good," he said. "You should think about the Air Force Academy." I'd put dreams on hold in Seattle. Now he reminded me I had possibilities.

Evenings and weekends were spent with Grandma. Family came and went, as always, but now she lived alone. After dinner, we played cards or watched TV. At ten we'd nudge her on the couch and she'd say, "I was just resting my eyes."

5.

Mom and Dad, meanwhile, were sleeping in a tent by the Elwha River. They'd used Gene's money to buy a '66 Jeep Wagoneer. (Gene said, "A '66?") Mom found a new job with the Social Security Administration. Port Angeles had drawn Mom and Dad with its small size, beautiful setting, and reputation for sunshine. This reputation derived from its lying in a "rain shadow" of the Olympic Mountains. That is, on the drier, leeward side.

Coming west, despite the tough time in Seattle, had been good for us. Getting away from Indiana gave Mom and Dad breathing room. It wasn't so politically conservative, they no longer felt themselves watched and judged, and Dad was able to find the occasional job. Not great ones (after the roofing job he worked at a methadone clinic), but things he could do without stressing out too much.

At summer's end, after Mom and Dad had found a house, Tracey and I got ready to rejoin them. Grandma took us shopping. As I slid a hanger on the rack, Grandma asked, "Do you think your mom would mind if I came with you to Washington?"

I glanced at her. I'd never heard her sound so vulnerable. And I honestly didn't know the answer. After Grandpa had died, Mom had not flown back to Indiana for the funeral, though Grandma had offered to buy the ticket. Mom's feelings had been still too raw. All she had ever tried to do was support her husband and keep her family intact. Why couldn't people understand that? Why couldn't they see in Dad the goodness she saw in him? No, going to the funeral would have been too painful for Mom, and to what end? It wouldn't bring Grandpa back.

A year later, though, it was different. Once again Grandma had helped us. Mom said yes.

At the Purdue airport Grandma took a picture of Tracey and me flanked by Gene and Margaret, their daughter Mary, and Grandma Mae. Though I did not know it at the time, that would be the last time we would ever see Gene and Margaret. In the photo we all smile and the sky is blue. Gene's bald head reminds me of the time Tracey asked if she could rub it. (She polished it like a bowling ball.) We hugged and said goodbye. I made sure to say thank you. I'd forgotten to do that when Gene bought me stamps and coins.

That was the first of many visits Grandma would make to Washington. From then on she came every other year, including us on the rotation of trips she made to see her kids and grandkids scattered around the country. When we got to Port Angeles, I was surprised to see Dad had cut his hair. I loved our new home from the start. The town was small, the weather was sunny, and yellow grass and fir trees lined the road.

Mom and Dad had started a garden. Seeing Dad at work, Grandma asked, "Do you want some help?" She got down on her hands and knees and began to weed. Watching them there, together in the dirt, Mom said, "That would never have happened in Indiana."

6.

In the fall of my senior year, I could afford three application fees. I requested forms from Stanford, Whitman, and Princeton.

Hearing I was applying to those schools, a mom on Bainbridge Island (where I attended a student exchange) asked, "What makes you think you can get into those schools?"

Because, I didn't say, *while your son has been bonking his Atari, I've been busting my ass. Because I'm student body president, have a 4.0, and am crushing the opposition in Lincoln-Douglas debate. Who are you to ask me this question?*

Which came to her ears as, "Well, my grades are good and the SAT went well, so I'm hopeful."

My reasons for picking those three were simple. Stanford, because it was excellent and kids from P.A. had been admitted in the past. Whitman, because it, too, was first-rate, and I was sure I could get in. And Princeton, because that was my idea of "going for it."

Princeton! I loved the very sound of it. It had the ring of an old phone, the important call coming in, the alert public servant standing at the ready. Yes, FDR and JFK had gone to Harvard, but JFK had started at Princeton, and Harvard was, after all, a tired cliché of strivers. Harvard had something haughty about it, and the banality of gold, but Princeton seemed to me more modest and serious. More suitable to daily use, like silver. Just look at who'd gone there: Adlai Stevenson, Bill Bradley, Jimmy Stewart! Brainy guys who were at the same time idealists and champions of the common man. I loved the common man!

7.

Or rather, I loved the idea of the common man. Many of the people around me drove me nuts. Later I would have to reconsider this matter from the perspective of faith, but at P.A. High I had been very glad to be fast-tracked out of classrooms in which "the rowdies"—that is, those for whom "Shrooms!" served as both a battle cry and source of giggle fits—were calling the shots.

Now, I'll grant you, some of those courses freshman year were spirit-killers. But one could at least make an effort, and from sophomore year on the available selection of courses improved significantly. Being fast-tracked in English, math, and other subjects made all the difference for me. After feeling lost and isolated my freshman year, I suddenly found myself surrounded by students who were equally motivated. By senior year my school day had turned into an extended session of arrogant banter, beginning with A.P. English in the morning, running through history and debate in the afternoon, and devolving into more free-form bullshitting in the evening hours.

A meditative intermezzo was provided by Mr. Kays' math class. John B. Kays drove a sports car with a radar detector, and sometimes he flew a Cessna to work from his home in Sequim. I guess that makes him sound like James Bond, but his cardigans undercut the image, and his quiet way reminded me more of Grandpa (who also was named John). Mr. Kays was kind and unassuming, a man of rectitude. Never once did he raise his voice in class. He didn't need to.

Boy, did I love doing proofs, sophomore year, in Mr. Kay's class! Geometry was math for the philosopher and wordsmith, a legal brief you handed in every day for the judge's review. Mr. Kays rose, glanced at us, and then drawing a perfect circle in a single motion. Bisecting it twice he'd point to the equal angles. "Do you see?"

One day I raised my hand. "Mr. Kays, what does the B stand for?"

He smiled and looked down. "Beldon," he said.

8.

My companions were the "A.P. crowd," a group of, on the whole, wholesome, bookish do-gooders. These were people who ran for student council, made homecoming floats, and hung up streamers for the dance. They, generally speaking, did not drink or smoke pot or stand in the hall spitting tobacco juice into a Coke can—the latter practice reflecting the timber culture of the Peninsula, where loggers (wearing boots and a hickory shirt) tucked a hockey-puck of "snoose" into a back pocket of their jeans. Now in my old age I have a nostalgic love for the history and practice of logging—I have several books on it in my "Ranger Station"—but I never did understand the appeal of saliva laced with tobacco juice, just as I could not see enjoying a joint wet from another's lips.

No, my friends and I were not out getting drunk on the weekends. Not at first anyway. Up until the halfway point of senior year we preferred the simple joys of pizza, football games, and the New Wave music that navigated the Scylla and Charybdis of Hard Rock and Disco. At my school in Seattle, Earth Wind and Fire had been the favorite band, but at P.A. High AC/DC ruled. I, for my part, joined my friends in their preference for The Police and The Cure (especially at dances: for you cannot dance to Rush's "Tom Sawyer"), but Nat King Cole was who I really loved. Nat of "Nature Boy" and "The Autumn Leaves." Nat who, when he sang "I'm Lost," stretched that syllable through the whole length of the wood. It was the combination of melancholy and reassurance that got me, and does to this day.

And so in the fall of '82 you'd have found us in the evening trying to light a fire at the pier, taking up once again the discussion we'd started that morning about London's *Sea-Wolf*—cross-referenced against Nietzsche and Ronald Reagan—and whether social Darwinism was reprehensible or the basis of society. Jim Heckman, my partner at debate tournaments, would not be there, for he ran with a faster crowd of jocks, but we would revisit the outrageous remarks he'd made in class, about supply-side and Jack Kemp (and what a great quarterback he'd been!) and about how you don't want your tax dollars keeping the riffraff in thrall to their own laziness ("The conglomerate you've built from the ground up, sweating blood for market share, and then some freeloader comes along for a paid vacation at your expense?! I don't think so!"). This prompting Fidler's interjection ("Now wait a minute!") and call for nuance, which in turn spurred the right-wingers Williams and Wyatt (I do them a disservice here: they were more moderate in position and tone) to come to Heckman's aid (Bilsborrow wondering meanwhile if we might not get back to the book itself), before I *dramatically*, appearing out of the dust as the Texas-Ranger-slash-voice-of-reason, rebut him: "My friends, yes, we can abandon the weak, seeing in their vulnerability a sign of God's or nature's rejection. But aren't all of us at some point, and inevitably in some fashion *weak*? Were Dust Bowlers who lost their farm victims of their own lack of industry? Sometimes life, through no fault of our own, deals us a dirty hand. Shouldn't we, when this happens, stand together? Aren't "We the People" about more than cutthroat, individualistic money-grabbing?" To which, I presumed, the class would rise in ovation. But instead my words generated only more hands raised in the quest for points in Mrs. Elliott's gradebook.

Ah well. But wow, fantastic, what fun!—going at it like that every weekday morning. They say kids don't read books anymore (mine hardly do) and that no one studies literature, but I loved how my English and debate classes launched discussions of what life is all about. And battling Heckman was a blast. For he was the best *and* the worst. The worst for being an aggressive bastard who, noting my skinny, pink tie, grabbed me by the throat, saying, "That's *my* tie!" (this being the same model he'd bought for himself at discount while working at Widsteen's)—and me laughing, thinking: *Ha ha, too late my friend!* Heckman, the loudmouth from freshman year who'd said I carried my books in an Adidas bag because I was "a fag."

And the best because *damn! at least he was alive.* He was going for it. He wasn't just sitting around pissing away his life. He thought about stuff, and took a stand and went after what he wanted. I respected that. And so despite our ideological differences (I overlooked the fact that even cavemen considered him reactionary) we were debate partners for a year, and we backed one another up at Boys' State and in the YMCA's Youth in Government program.

In the evenings, though, we went our separate ways. I settled in again with my laid-back friends. Basden finally got that fire lit. A seagull dipped. You could hear the water lapping and smell the seaweed. The talk turned to the drama class's production of *The Music Man.* They sang a few numbers. When it got too cold, we left the glowing coals for coffee at Haguewood's. From our table I'd have liked to search the twilight through the window, but at that hour all the window gave was my own reflection.

9.

Not pissing away one's life was a big issue for me. For death awaited and life was flying by. You had to squeeze all the juice out of it while you could, which meant refusing any notion of God or an afterlife. Such beliefs kept you from seizing the only thing that was truly available, the here and now. "Death is the mother of beauty," I'd say.

Which annoyed Katie. "I don't want to think about death all day. What does a poet know anyway?"

"It's reality. You want to live in the real world, don't you?"

"Thinking about death all the time isn't living," she said, "it's miserable."

"Well, you don't have to actually think about it. You don't have to stare at a skull all day. You just need to have the awareness underwriting everything you do."

She eyed me skeptically. "Why are you so dark? Mister, you need to lighten up."

And seeing her curves and ample willingness, I conceded she had a point. Death was a drag. So I went back to nibbling at her neck. *Carpe diem.*

What had first made death really sink in was the horrible fate of Gene and Margaret. Less than a year after we left them, we got a call from Grandma Mae. Margaret had shot Gene in the back and herself in the head. Gene had been having an affair.

That night, while tears ran from my eyes, I imagined it all. I knew their house so well, even knew where the safe was hidden. I saw Margaret take the gun and stash it in a hamper. I saw Gene undress, remove his shoes, unbutton his shirt. I saw Margaret pointing the gun. Mostly, though, I saw the blood, which became the red light of lurid dreaming.

When we'd been with them I'd sensed no tension, had seen no indication whatsoever that their marriage was on the rocks. Losing Grandpa had made me sad, but I got it. He smoked too much. But why did this have to happen?

After that, death was no longer an abstraction. It was vividly present, and its power lay, terrifyingly, in our hands.

10.

But whether I thought it should be or not, death wasn't always on my mind. Indeed, as my senior year progressed, thoughts of death evaporated like a puddle in the sun, the sun being my nuclear-powered love of girls. Angst stood no chance against that. Women were everywhere, a daily diversion. All I needed, I thought, was to find the one-and-only, true ultimate goddess and all my problems would be solved.

But where was she?

I mean, it was pretty clear how it was supposed to go. It would start with the rustling of leaves on a bracing day in September. She'd be strikingly beautiful, but not in an intimidating way. She'd be shy but smart. She'd be wholesome. She wouldn't have any issues at home. (I had enough for two.) She'd brighten when I asked her to the dance. On the day of, I'd drive by myself out to the lake, which would be the blue-green of a crayon. There I would imagine and savor the evening ahead, the slow unfolding capped by a single kiss. And then all that would actually happen.

Was it too much to ask?

Unfortunately, I kept botching it. At the time, my failures were a mystery to me, but over the years, I've gained insight into why one might have resisted or dumped me.

There was, for one thing, my approach, which relied heavily on verbal pyrotechnics. These left the girl, typically, mystified. Instead of just saying hi, for example, I'd write her a note. "If you were ice-cream, you'd be French-vanilla." Which was my way of saying: "You are creamy-delicious and evocative. Shall we get together?"

But she didn't get that. Her girlfriend, having seen the note, acknowledged my point: "You're right, that would be the flavor." But it didn't get me any closer to a date.

Such indirectness led to a rebuke in my annual. A girl with whom it hadn't worked out wrote: "It's so important just to be yourself."

But what the hell? Wasn't this beauty-bedazzled, loquacious fireball *exactly* who I was? Wasn't it exactly who I was *in spades*?

Be yourself. Whatever.

So repeatedly I stranded in what I, in my future work, would learn to call the "Courtyard of the Gentiles." That is, at the outermost part of the Temple, far removed from the Holy of Holies.

There I would enjoy a conversation with the girl's best friend, with whom I *did* hit it off. She would be straightforward and funny, and typically this click made the girl in question (the object of my desire) see what a great couple her friend and I would make. And she'd want this for us (even though that's not what I wanted), and out of love for her friend she wouldn't want to get in our way. So she'd withdraw yet further, deeper within the sanctuary.

This stuff is all in the movies. I've seen my missteps played out a thousand times. My advice: Watch the movies first.

So there I was, midway through senior year, with no true love in sight. That said, there *was* a very shapely gal in my typing class. But that was pure lust.

11.

On the home front, things had settled down considerably. Dad worked for a time at a bike shop, accepting it peacefully when it ended. What drama there was revolved around Tracey. She was often at odds with Mom and Dad. I stayed out of it. All the emotion and discussion seemed a waste of energy to me. Frankly, at that point I couldn't relate to any of them. Not to Dad because he so often had been a mystery to me and source of frustration. Not to Mom because, while I understood why she'd stayed with Dad, her preoccupation with his struggles left her less present to me. And not to Tracey because her rebellion against authority and attraction to stoners appalled me. It was as if she took being down-and-out to be a self-evidently superior moral position. I drove her wild when I put a good word in for "conformity" (as I did Mom and Dad when I said the "silent majority" also had a point). So Tracey and I ignored one another, limiting our battles to those arising from the single shared bathroom. These reduced to me telling her to get out, her taunting me from within ("If you want it, you'll have to beg"), and me calling her a "skag."

12.

By my junior year (according to my plan) I should have made All-State in basketball. But that was actually when I quit. I joined the debate team instead. When I asked Coach Burtness if I'd ever be able to miss a ballgame for a debate tournament, he said, "No."

It was a relief, really. I'd ridden the bench for two years, and playing ball out west had never worked out. In Seattle they played a variety of run-and-gun rat-ball that didn't sit well with me, and in Port Angeles I'd realized I had decent skills (I could give you a textbook description of how to shoot a free throw), but lacked court sense and aggression. I failed to anticipate the open man, and too often when I did see him I'd telegraph my pass. This short-coming taught me something valuable, though. I saw you could be smart in different ways. There were guys who were duds in class, who were smoking me on the hardwoods. *C'est la vie.*

Now debate, that was playing to my strength. Research, speechifying, that I could do. And there were a lot of smart girls running around at tournaments, some of whom were pretty good looking. Our team competed once or twice a month, taking off on Friday or Saturday, depending on the distance to be traveled. Port Angeles was isolated—there was only one highway connecting us to the rest of the world—and the isolation was even more pronounced my first three years. In 1979 the Hood Canal bridge had blown out in a storm, so even to get to the Kitsap Peninsula, where other schools in our league were, you had to take a ferry. And if you were going to Seattle, you had catch another one after that. But ferries were part of the fun: clambering up the stairs, taking coffee to the deck, enjoying the salt air and jabber, and then hustling back when the horn sounded. Returned to the van, we resumed our slow progress, with Heckman explaining the "genius" of Led Zeppelin and/or why socialist France should be kicked out NATO, Wyatt giving answer, and me saying that shit wasn't worth an answer. Mrs. Hall, our coach and first red-headed English teacher at P.A. High (Mrs. Elliott was our second) would approach our exchange philosophically, saying perhaps it wasn't so cut and dried as all that, but then giggle knowing we weren't interested in subtleties. Eventually we shut up and retreated into our Walkmans.

At tournaments I competed in Lincoln-Douglas, the more laid-back, rhetorically beautiful style of debate I'd turned to after sickening of the data-and-spit-spewing, card file mania of cross-ex. Heckman and I had done that the previous year, but winning in cross-x seemed to be based more on the speed of discourse and the size of one's card file than on actual skills of persuasion. (Some dudes needed a dolly to drag their cards around.) Lincoln-Douglas was better if you actually liked language and believed in the exchange of ideas.

Besides debate, I got my jollies in the YMCA's Youth in Government program. There we spent the year preparing for the mock legislature held in Olympia in the spring. Port Angeles had an especially strong delegation that year, comprised of many I knew from class and the debate team. Among them was a promising underclassmen, Sung Yang. I met Sung at just the right time.

13.

I first spoke with Sung during the intermission of a dance at the City Gym. He and another young debater, Jack Rappaport, were just back from a tournament I'd skipped. I'd needed to take the ACT. "How'd it go?" I asked.

"It was a debacle," Sung said. "We sailed through the early rounds and were scorching those guys from Olympia—I'd just wrapped it up, raising, I swear, for the third time our point about F-16's—we were a short putt away from a trophy—when the judge dogged us. On the ballot he said we didn't bring up F-16's until rebuttals, but I totally did in second neg. A travesty."

"Harsh," I said.

Rappaport nodded. "Shady. Douche was asleep at the wheel."

"And oh yeah," Sung said, "Wyatt used the 'Read my lips' card."

"You're kidding! Damn. *I* wanted to use that card." We'd been saving the card, which had a smooch imprinted on the front, above the words "Read my lips." We thought it would be the perfect opening gambit with some lissome fox. Whoever saw her first was allowed to use it. Now Wyatt had gotten the jump on us (the bastard). Whether it had had the desired effect, was unclear, but it was definitely a pisser that he'd beaten us to the punch with a girl who, from Sung's description, sounded well worth one's while. Anyway.

The more I spoke with Sung, the more I liked him. Him and Rappaport both. We all stood at approximately the same ironical remove.

Turning to the action at hand, I noted that it had been lame so far. The low point had come right before the break. "When she asked me, I said, 'Sure' (thinking let's just get this over with and at least she's not snapping her gum like she does in class), but then it turned out to be a slow dance, and not just any slow dance, but the most endless and tragic of all slow dances, "Stairway to Heaven." That shit goes on forever! One good thing, though. Halfway through, just as the boys were breaking out their air guitars, I spotted the Bo Derek of my typing class giving me the eye. Oh yeah she was. You know it. We've got something cooking and I can't wait to taste it. Now there is a girl who's bountifully endowed! She's into me, I'm tellin' ya."

"Nice to know," Sung said. "Where is she now?"

We looked around.

"Good question. Maybe she has a curfew or something."

A more thorough scan of the field revealed precious few targets for the second set.

"Well, boys, should we get out of here? I hear they make an excellent cinnamon roll down at Haguewood's. Maybe that's where everyone is."

"Sure," they said, "I got nothin' goin'."

14.

After that I looked for Sung at tournaments and in the student center at school. It turned out we had a lot in common. An interest in politics, for one. Sung appreciated, as I did, that in politics power and style went together. The look and sound of things went far in determining whether power was acquired and goals attained; and we were fascinated by how that played out specifically in practice. We differed as to what style was to be preferred—Sung, for example, being a Reagan man, tied those old-fogey Windsor knots, whereas I preferred JFK's crisp four-in-hand. But we were one in our fascination with how Reagan or Churchill or whomever used words, images and their own charisma to "move the masses." That's what we aspired to do ourselves.

Mostly, though, Sung was easy to be around. He was at once laid-back and driven. Before that I hadn't hung out with any particular person, except for Ronaldo, another guard on the basketball team (who unlike me did not pee his pants when the other team threw down a full-court press). But now I started dropping by Sung's place to assess with him the latest OMD and/or Human League and/or Stray Cats video on MTV. Sung's parents owned the comically-named Royal Victorian motel (neither royal nor Victorian; though to be fair, Sung's parents had not named it, they'd simply bought it, in the move that had brought them to town). After a while Rappaport would show up. Like Sung, Jack was a recent arrival in P.A., in his case from New York after his parents bought the local health food shop, "The Country Aire" (yes, with an E). The three of us were all, though we never spoke of it openly, outsiders in town—not only because we were relative newcomers, but also because Sung (South Korean by birth) was one of only a very few Asians and Jack was one of the very few Jews. I for my part felt cut off because Dad's troubles kept our family turned in upon itself. Chris Koenig, the fourth in our circle, was the only one who seemed fully at home in P.A. He'd grown up there, and his dad owned the local Chevy dealership. Chris shuttled us around in a late-edition Blazer, regularly crying abuse of "Chris's taxi service." By the time he showed up, there'd be no room on the couch, so he'd have to pull up a chair.

Once we settled in, Mrs. Yang brought pizza. This stirred Jack's recollection of the time he got robbed of a pizza in New York. "I was walking home with it and this guy came up and said, 'Gimme that pizza' and then he popped me in the mouth."

For some reason we all thought this was funny. We said, "You must be so glad you live in P.A."

But no, Jack had very mixed feelings about P.A.

15.

My friendship with Sung might have amounted only to a few months of biding time and yucking it up—I was leaving for college soon—but it turned out I could relate to him on a deeper level. I first realized this on a debate trip. As we barreled down the empty stretch between Sequim and Discovery Bay, Mrs. Hall discovered she'd left her purse at home. Going back would cost an hour, so she decided to press on. I was glad, because we were headed to Lower Columbia College and it was going to be a long-enough trip already. At dinner that night, Sung asked her if she needed money. And then he snuck off to order her desert, for she'd mentioned it was her anniversary. If I'd thought Sung had a thing for Mrs. Hall or was just working on his grade, I'd have thought, *Give me a break.* But I knew it wasn't that. He was just being kind in a way I wished I'd managed to be. I thought, *That's a class act.*

Later he quoted Eleanor Roosevelt to me: "When you cease to make a contribution, you begin to die." When he said that I realized politics was for him, as it was for me, about more than just raising your own profile. It was about service. And peace and justice. It was about seeing the harsh reality and doing something about it. I often had in mind an image of Robert Kennedy down in Mississippi in '67, seeing those poor kids, how that burdened him. You can't just close your eyes to it. You can't just walk away from it and do nothing. Politics should bring change for the better.

Even student government, the stuff we were doing. Yes, we were playing at it. We were learning the political system. But I saw we could also address real issues. I hated the bake-sale philosophy of student government—that reduction of it all to car washes and pennyante fundraisers to earn money for the dance. Why not think big? Why not do something that mattered? Granted, dances mattered—to my fellow students, and to me as well (I loved them: thank God Vice President Amy organized Homecoming)—but you could do more than that. And that's what I'd proposed we do, in what I wrote in the student guidebook handed out at the start of the year. In the course of the year I wanted to make sure we got some of that done. So we held a blood drive, raised money for a scholarship, and organized a dinner for senior citizens.

Yeah I got misty eyed when it came to "ideals." I watched those old movies and took them for the Gospel truth: Jimmy Stewart as "Mr. Smith," filibustering against corruption on the floor of the Senate, and putting it to old-man Potter in *It's a Wonderful Life*: "This rabble you're talking about, they do most of the working and paying and living and dying in this community." And don't even get me started on *The Paper Chase*, my favorite show—about Professor Kingsfield and law student Hart, with his "wholehearted, indivisible commitment to humanity."

Sung was less gushy about this stuff than I was, but he knew what I was talking about and could relate. So the friendship transcended and outlasted the jokey nonsense of the spring of 1983.

16.

I still have the journal I kept that year, and almost all I've written since. Upon rereading that very first one, what stands out is the number of four- and five-star days—what a carefree and exciting year that was—and even more, my obsession with girls. One damsel after another captivated me. Several times I lament a failure with one at the top of the page and transition seamlessly into praise of the next by the bottom. I'll spare you the names, rhapsody, and distress but now I stand amazed: what a depth of need, so deep and so strong!

17.

I got ever looser over the course of the year. After having once told Katie that I was never going to drink, I sampled and developed a taste for champagne. On New Year's Eve I supplied a party with it and made sure I got my share. At 2:00 a.m. on the first day of 1983 I found myself drunk on my ass on the floor of Jenny Chamberlain's basement. Her mom walked in and said, "Well well, our illustrious student body president." Jenny's boyfriend drove me home. In the morning, Mom was surprised to hear me puking. Later Jenny told me I'd been quoting the Constitution.

So yes, on occasion, when given the opportunity, I got toasted. I even skipped class a time or two, though not quite as boldly as Heckman, who simply climbed out the open window of Burtness's computer science class. I wasn't willing to do anything that might jeopardize my G.P.A. I'd worked too hard to get where I was, and the time of reckoning was at hand.

18.

And then, just as my exhilarating year was coming to an end, I met her.

I'd seen her before but now she made an impression on me. She did it by beating me on a math quiz. Mr. Kays used to invite whoever wanted to to come in at lunch and solve some puzzles. It was a standardized thing called the Atlantic-Pacific test. You had twenty minutes to solve five problems. The first time we did it she got three right to my one. Afterwards I said, Who is this?

I bought her a banana split for beating me. Over the ice-cream I asked her, "So who's your favorite President?"

"FDR," she said.

FDR! I couldn't believe it.

Most kids at our school had never even heard of FDR. And the only one who ever talked about him was Kathy Williams, who was always giving me crap about the internment camps and him being sick at Yalta and "selling out Eastern Europe."

"Why FDR?" Oh I don't know. Because he wore those little glasses. And he got the country through the war and the Great Depression."

"Wow," I said. "I love FDR." (I *did* love FDR. I loved his grin and the fireside chats and the Four Freedoms. Next to JFK throwing touchdowns on the White House lawn, FDR at the wheel of an open car was my favorite image of a President.) I said, "He came here once, you know. To P.A. In '37. A year later he established the national park. Before that it had been a national monument, which his cousin Teddy had set aside."

"Well I did not know that," she said.

Then I plied her with questions and saw her mind went places I didn't expect, by means of words I did not expect. Like *aorta*. Which arose from a corny joke she made, pulling a voice, saying "I orta clobber you!" That led her to ask if I knew what an aorta was.

"It's part of the heart," I said, "but biology is not my strong suit."

"Well let me show you." She borrowed a pen from the waitress and started to draw on the napkin. "This is the superior vena cava…"

Anyway, that's sort of how it went. I don't remember exactly, just remember the way she was. I took a good look at her. She had brown eyes and an upbeat, healthy glow about her. It was too bad she was two years younger. But she had a future, for sure. I'd have to keep tabs on her. Suzanne. Suzanne Turner.

19.

When I think of that spring, I think of dominoes falling, those being the prizes that fell one after another at my feet. Granted, I didn't place first at state debate. After sweeping the ballots through the early rounds, I finished sixth, losing to a girl from Gonzaga Prep in the quarterfinals. But when I got home from the tournament, Tracey told me someone from Whitman had called. I'd won their top scholarship, a full ride. They would fly me over to have dinner with the president and tour the campus.

Earlier that week my picture had been in the paper. Our Knowledge Bowl team had won the regional competition. (I noted with pleasure the words: "Then Schilling provided an invincible edge…")

Ten days after hearing from Whitman, I received a letter from Stanford. Sick with fear I opened it. Probably somewhere I still have that letter ("We are pleased to inform you…"). God Almighty! Unbelievable.

At the youth legislature in Olympia, I was voted "Outstanding Senator." And then the Port Angeles Rotary named me "Boy of the Year."

But the top prize and greatest joy came on April 18th. It was strange to think, as I held that letter, that I might in a minute be "disappointed to be going to Stanford." Three years earlier, the thought of my going there would have been thrilling. But now I had this other idea stuck in my head. Princeton was where I really wanted to go, and if I didn't get in, I would, I knew, for all my success, feel a little like a failure (sad as that sounds to me now). I slit open the envelope.

Seeing the acceptance, I got down on my knees and put my head on the floor.

20.

There are times in life when time itself slows down and expands, allowing within it a leisure previously unknown. That's how it was through the rest of that spring and on into the summer. Having ramped it up over the last two years—squeezing my shifts at Albertson's in between classes, debate, student government, and homework—I found myself now graduated, with little work to do and no immediate worries about the future. A dreaminess entered in. I savored hot showers and stretches of working on nothing but my tan. To feel productive, I called Sung, who was always glad to play tennis. Doubles, I insisted, because it was more sociable and I didn't want to run. I'd had enough of that for a while. In the evening I wandered down to the library, to look at *Esquire* or read up on the wonders of law school.

On occasion I talked Sung into going with me to Suzanne's. The pretext was finding her brother Lee, another friend of ours, a center on the basketball team. The Turners had a big house at the edge of town, with a hoop and tennis court, and a shed for skis. Beyond the tennis court lay the garden, the pasture, and the Olympic mountains.

After a game of HORSE, we adjourned to the kitchen. Mrs. Turner poured lemonade. I knew who she was before I met her.

Her picture had recently been on the front page of the *Seattle P-I* after she'd thwarted Northern Tier's plan to turn Port Angeles into an oil port. They'd wanted to ship crude from Alaska and send it through a pipeline on to the rest of the country. Though Reagan had backed the plan, Mrs. Turner and a team of local activists had stood up for the environmental and local quality-of-life interests. I was eager to hear all about the victory.

When Suzanne walked in, she said, "Well, Mr. Schilling. What brings you here?"

That summer I went there whenever I politely could. There was always something baking—some crisp with berries from the yard—and Suzanne's dad, a pediatrician, was always up for tennis. Suzanne by now was aware I was smitten with her, though I never said that in so many words. (Or did I? What *did* I say in my notes to her and in her annual?) The way I saw it: she was fit, she was funny, she was fine. Or as *Esquire* put it: "She had the legs, heart and bloodline of a champion." So what if she was too young? I could wait.

21.

My evening walks, ostensibly to the library, became ends in themselves. When I was inclined to stop, I got a coffee across from the courthouse. More often, though, I stepped inside churches. They were always open and you could sit in silence. My favorite was St. Andrew's, Mr. Kays' church. In the dim light I imagined him there. It was funny to be in a church. Through my high school years I'd been a fiery atheist. Now, though, I was less vehement. This had started when Suzanne had said, "How can you be so sure there's no God?"

If it had been anyone else, I'd have rattled off a list of answers. But since *she'd* said it, I thought: "She's right. How can I be so sure?"

Princeton

Looking back now, I wonder how much time I spent looking for the Princeton I thought I would find. Or meant to find. That leafy, bookish, girl-in-cashmere-sweater Princeton. That place of arches and beveled glass in tall windows. These particulars were there, of course, but the finding of them never quite conjured the sensation I had anticipated. An acapella group singing under a tree bough in the moonlight can be just one more thing you pass on your way home from the library. But I seized on such details in my early letters home, and indeed went actively in search of them during long walks on campus. On stationery adorned with the Princeton shield (in lines perfectly straight on unlined paper) I shared that I had ridden from the airport in a limousine (together with three other students and our huge pile of luggage); that I now lived in what had been an inn, in a room overlooking a golf course; that Nassau Hall had once housed the Continental Congress; that I'd met a guy who'd scored a double-800 on his SAT; and that yes, I had seen Brooke Shields (who was in my class) numerous times. Besides these noteworthy items, I also passed on photographs, bumper stickers, t-shirts, and sweatshirts to my friends back in P.A. So they'd know I was really there. And so they wouldn't forget me.

My favorite discovery was the Adlai Stevenson window in a corner of the chapel. Adlai, the intellectual, the man of peace, the statesman! An accompanying text quoted the first Psalm: "He is like a tree planted near running water, that yields its fruit in due season." Besides being a fan of Adlai, I also had a thing for trees. I was glad to be back among the deciduous. For much as I loved the conifers of the Northwest, I missed the changing, falling leaves of my boyhood years. On Saturday afternoons I went out to be with them—along College Road to Battle Road and out around the Institute for Advanced Study. The ash and elm trees stood silently. They were not rushing around. They were not wanting.

2.

I signed up for calculus, American foreign policy, European history, and Spanish. But the first problem set convinced me that calculus was not a good idea. In high school the opening months were usually a review of what I already knew, but here I reached the limit of my knowledge almost immediately. Solving those first problems took forever, so I took Shakespeare instead. My second course-change was occasioned by a mistake. Thinking I was sitting down to a foreign policy lecture, I was surprised to see a dude in cowboy boots stroll out. He started talking about Russia in 1905. It was electric, bringing to mind Abby Hoffman's words: "The revolution is where my boots hit." So I dropped foreign policy in favor of Professor Cohen's Soviet Politics course.

Joining me in getting settled was my roommate, Ramon McGee. Having seen his name before I arrived, I'd wondered: Is he Irish? Hispanic? He turned out to be a tall Black guy from Maryland. He'd run track for Georgetown Prep but then passed on a scholarship to Villanova to go to Princeton. He rocked. He was very easy-going, and when he laughed, the whole place shook. One time his twin sister Ramona visited and they kept me up all night. I was jealous of how loose and joyous they were. Ramon was super enthusiastic. When I had little successes—like an A on my first paper in Shakespeare—he was happier for me than I was, high-fiving me and slapping me on the back. "All Right!!!"

We did the standard stuff getting acclimated: taking the tour, meeting advisors, going to mixers, the football game. We lived at Princeton Inn College (P.I.C.), one of the five residential colleges, in the last year before it became Forbes College. It was good.

People were nice. In Green Hall I met my new boss. As part of my financial aid package, I'd been assigned to work in the psychology library. Soon thereafter I joined the Princeton Democrats. They were led by two sons of Senator Paul Sarbanes of Maryland. Our focus that year was on re-electing Princeton's Mayor, Barbara Boggs-Sigmund, and working on the Presidential campaign. John Schachter would be speaking with those who wanted to campaign for Gary Hart. Hart was the man, I thought. He had a much better chance of bringing down Reagan than Mondale did. Hart—young and charismatic, with his "new ideas."

But still, Princeton wasn't home, so Ramon and I were always hopeful of receiving letters and ideally a care package. The mail came—when it came—right around lunchtime. We stopped on our way to the cafeteria, turning the key to open the little box in the wall full of them.

In my best stretch I received personal mail forty days in a row. That was my payoff for being a writing machine. Every night after finishing the assigned reading, I wrote letters. To everyone, but especially to Suzanne. And she wrote to me. Cheery, hopeful letters. But not from Port Angeles. From Vermont. Her dad was working there for a year so the family could explore the East Coast. They'd bought a condo, she liked her school.

Before I'd left Port Angeles, Mrs. Turner had said: "You're welcome to join us for Thanksgiving." I couldn't believe she offered. That would be, I thought, the greatest thing ever.

3.

On my second Sunday in Princeton I knotted my tie and asked Ramon, "You want to go?"

"No thanks."

Frederick Borsch, the dean of the chapel, led us in prayer. He would later serve as the Episcopal bishop of Los Angeles. He was to my mind the very picture of a Princeton-and-Oxford-educated priest. His eyes and voice and mind were clear.

I felt welcome. I sang the hymns. I admired the windows. But I felt out of place. It was as if I were play-acting. Once was enough.

4.

A more sturdy, hardcover journal replaced my spiral notebook of the previous year. Once the weather got cool (and I could finally wear the sweaters I'd bought), I began jotting down a "Christmas quote" at the start of every entry. These I lifted from Dickens or Bartlett or Bing Crosby. I was already looking ahead to the holidays, for that to me was the time of romance. Advent was for serene dreaminess and falling in love.

I've kept a journal for forty years now. I still have all of them but that one. In the summer of '92 I popped open its three rings and dumped its pages in the garbage. It was so over-the-top, so desperate. Maybe it's for the best. Some mysteries are disserved by words.

But let's just cut to the chase, shall we?

5.

It started with silence. With Suzanne's that is, with the drying up of the stream of letters.

What could it mean? She was, naturally, busy with her new school, and I didn't expect her to write me as often as I wrote her. And letters could be delayed enroute, which might explain why there was nothing from her on any given day.

But still, something had changed.

We just need to be together is all.

6.

A girl on my hall listened skeptically as I went on about Kennedy. She said, "Have you ever read *The Best and the Brightest*?"

I checked out a copy, but quickly lost patience with Halberstam. He was so cynical. Why so suspicious? Why not take the high-mindedness of Kennedy and his men at face value? Ironically, while annoyed with Halberstam's tone, I also thrilled to his detailing of Rusk's and McNamara's and Sorenson's background and credentials. These were helpful blueprints, much as the *Preppie Handbook* taught hicks how to dress. (When a girl back in P.A. saw I hadn't put pennies in my loafers, she joked, "Tim, they'll know . . ."). I was willing to grant the point about hubris leading men astray, but if not the best and brightest, who *should* call the shots?

7.

I boarded the bus for Vermont on the day before Thanksgiving. The trip took most of the day. By five the sky had deepened to violet. The driver clicked on his lights.

Had it snowed? Maybe a little. The year before, back on the Peninsula, I'd gotten Ronaldo to drive us up the Ridge Road in search of it. We'd found some at Lake Dawn.

South of Burlington we passed a sign on a butcher shop: "Fresh killed deer."

Lee picked me up at the station. "There he is," he said, "our bedraggled world traveler."

"I hear we're going to watch you play."

"Yes, that's what they tell me. Well, we're not too bad. Not too good, but not too bad."

8.

Almost everything was perfect. We played board games and ate turkey. On Friday the snow fell. Shelley made cookies and Andrew, Lee, and I threw snowballs. Lee scored a dozen in a winning effort. I felt lucky to be the only guest. (After the oil port victory, the Turners had had seventy-five in to celebrate.)

On Saturday the sun came out. We drove to Montreal, to skate on Lake Champlain. On the drive back I passed forward my Johnny Mathis tape. "Wild Is the Wind" perfectly captured my love for Suzanne. Lee said, "Oh my God."

Suzanne wasn't impressed either. She kept the silence she'd begun in her letters.

So when I said "almost perfect," I meant: almost except for the gaping hole in the middle of the weekend that was bigger than the weekend itself.

I didn't get it. Where had it gone wrong? And more importantly, how could I fix it?

9.

I seized my one chance to speak with her alone. I followed Suzanne to her room and sat opposite her in the closet where she slept, on a mattress on the floor.

"It's just," she said, "I don't know."

"No, there's no one else."

I have, somewhere in a box, a photo her dad took. We stand before Lake Champlain. Her hair is a mess of curls. I smile but she frowns.

10.

As soon as I got back to Princeton I wrote her: "I totally understand."

I'll prove my love, I thought. *I can wait. We love the one who loves us most—don't we?*

I worked my shifts at the library and read *Tender Is the Night*. It got colder. Lights went on in the pretty shops. I bought cards and asked to see the selection of stamps. I would be heading home for Christmas soon. Suzanne wouldn't be there, but everyone else would. Sung and I were going to throw a very big party.

11.

For three weeks I heard nothing. Then it arrived, right before I left. She'd put her hand to it, licked the fold, pressed the stamp with her thumb. She'd dropped it in a box and a man had retrieved it. He'd taken it to a vast room where it had passed through all sorts of marvelous sorting mechanisms. From there it had proceeded south by plane and by truck to my residence, an inn on a golf course at a historic university—and specifically to the one slot assigned to me.

I opened it. It bore a flame of hope—a wavering flame, slender and lithe as a dancer.

12.

I took all I might possibly need, even my boom box. Grandma had bought me a round-trip ticket (Port Angeles-Newark) when I'd graduated. Now I used the return. The best part was the final leg, in the eight-seater in the dark, with the Strait below and the Olympics to my left. I could see the Peninsula, but couldn't see into it. Which was fitting, for it had been one of the last parts of the country to be explored. Not until 1885 had white men entered and reported back on the interior, and even Indians, I'd read, held back from the innermost domain. That was where the Thunderbird lived.

13.

When I visited the high school, it was just as I'd imagined. I bounded up the steps two at a time and walked in to Mrs. Elliott's wearing cuffed charcoal trousers and a blue blazer. I sat on a desk, waxing philosophical with her seniors. It was an old tradition at P.A. High: the big shots coming back from their first year of college. I'd watched Sleeper do it, just back from Macalaster. I'd thought, *What's with the scarf? You'd have to be an arrogant dick to wear that.* But now I thought, *Who cares what they think?*

When I saw Mr. Kays, he asked, "Are you taking calculus?"

It was great to be back. I was so psyched. I spent all my time with Sung and Jack. Christmas Eve and Christmas Day were about the only times I saw Mom and Dad. When I left I felt guilty.

14.

Word got around about the party. Mom and Dad now lived in a two-story place on Mount Angeles Road. To my delight they offered to sleep elsewhere on New Year's Eve.

Whoo boy, *everyone* came. Girls from Sung's class, people from mine, Heckman, Suits—even Katie showed up. And best of all, that girl from my typing class, who had the hottest body, and to whom I'd once complained, in passing, that it was a shame we'd never gotten together.

Not that I had any plans in that regard. I mean, I was going to be faithful to Suzanne. That was all there was to it. That was all that mattered. But I did intend to enjoy myself. So by the time people started arriving, I was already rolling on rum and Coke. When Suzanne's friend Christy pulled up, I ran down and did a drum roll on the hood of her mom's car. Strangely enough, when you're young and drunk, you think other people can't tell you're drunk.

Her mom kindly ignored it. "I'll come get you at one," she said.

As she drove away I hucked a penny up at Koenig, who stood inside looking out our plate glass window. The next day Mom and Dad would find that penny upright on the windowsill, together with the broken chair inside, and the confetti our vacuum hadn't managed to retrieve.

When the ball dropped in New York, Jack handed me a cigar. "Excellent," I said. I set my glass down and went to look for a match. As I turned to return from our refurbished basement, I saw I wasn't alone. The perfect temptress had followed.

"What's up?" she said.

I said, "Well, I was just about to light this cigar."

And then amazingly, maturely, boldly, she brushed it aside. She put her arms around my neck and looked up into my eyes.

She was like a present, the last best gift of Christmas.

Well well well.

I eased her back her down onto the couch. I started to open my present.

15.

Three days later, from the bus station in Missoula, Montana, I sent Suzanne a mailgram. Just to say hello.

I was in the middle of what would prove to be a four-and-a-half day trip. In the snow it took 24 hours to get across Montana alone. Now that I was footing the bill myself, this was the one way I could afford: $69 on Greyhound.

When I got back to school I found a letter from Suzanne waiting.

She'd already heard.

"It's better this way," she said.

16.

The place we enter now is a narrow passageway that eventually offers no passage at all. Sometimes I wonder how it came to that. For how many guys did I know—how many girls—who'd easily walked away from the same situation—indeed, didn't even see it as a problem? Hooking up, making out, having a little fun—the very language we use to describe it suggests how inconsequential we take it to be. One "gets lucky" or, more blandly, "gets some," and walks away.

The funny thing in this particular case is that I didn't even *get any* in the usual sense. There would be little of what I would later halfway regret I'd missed.

What I did enjoy in that moment was a kiss, and delight in her attraction, and the delicious anticipation of reveling in her body—sensations cut short by Jack's clambering down, wondering what was keeping me and those matches. I stood and fled the enticing girl. Seeing Katie, I implored, "Save me!" She joined me in a locked room, which was not exactly a solution to the problem.

Afterwards Katie thought it was all quite funny.

17.

The final exam for Soviet Politics was a ten-page paper due at the end of January. In preparation for the European history exam, I made myself a timeline, taping sheets of paper end-to-end. All Ramon and I did that month was carbo-load and study. During the day, anyway. At night I lay awake wondering how I could have blown it, the one thing I wanted more than anything.

I wrote to Sung. I wrote to Christy. I talked it over with Ramon and whomever would listen. What should I do?

The trees were black lines, reaching for the sky. Where was the "moving on"? Where was the ability I'd had in high school to fail with one girl and refocus, within hours, on the next? Why did all this talking-it-over not lead to dissipation of the problem?

How would I ever be faithful to my wife, if I hadn't been faithful to Suzanne?

I couldn't live up to my own ideals.

18.

In the second week of February, Dad congratulated me: "Those are really good grades." I'd scored A's in Shakespeare and Spanish, an A- in Soviet Politics, and a B+ in European History. I'd proved I could do it, a kid from the sticks.

But I was exhausted. Why was I doing this? What was the point? To get into law school and work even harder? I dreaded the thought of it. Friends from Port Angeles said, "When you're in the Senate . . ."

Crossing Alexander, I saw how precarious life is. A car could hit me and it would be over. And not just me: the universe itself. For if I can't experience it, does it matter if it exists at all?

19.

There must surely be, I thought, a book. During my shift at the psychology library I saw one: *Man's Search for Meaning*, by Viktor Frankl. *That's what I need, meaning.*

I pulled it from the stacks. I hoped he would tell me what to believe and what to do.

But he didn't.

What I didn't want was to make my own meaning. I'd tried that already: generating ideals and pep-talking myself into living them out.

No, I wanted *the* meaning, universal meaning, solid ground.

20.

My life was flying by, it was getting away from me. I tried sleeping less. (*If I sleep an hour less a night, it will add years to my life . . .*) But I kept falling asleep.

I read *The Sound and the Fury*. I could totally relate to Quentin Compson—to his murky despair and all those ticking clocks. "I give it to you not that you may remember time, but that you might forget it now and then for a moment and not spend all your breath trying to conquer it."

Later a psychologist would throw into his report the term "suicidal ideation." *Bogus!* I thought. That was the last thing I would do. I was deathly afraid of death. Even torture, I thought, would be better than death, for death was just nothing—nothing at all forever.

21.

At least the problems in my childhood "Why?" poem had been problems I could point to. But what do you do when you yourself are the problem? I sat in the chapel as the light dimmed. I went round and round. Love is just chemicals. No, less than that: atoms, subatomic particles, ever-smaller bits going down to nothing. The whole cosmos a sandstorm of nothing. I didn't cohere enough even to perceive it.

A well opened up within me. I fell into the well. Its wall was smooth, an endless wall. The circle above me shrank. I sank but I smiled—"No, I haven't . . . Yes, I am . . . "

I showered and shaved and worked my shift—and didn't care, or did, or didn't know.

Pop songs sickened me. "You are everything and everything is you." But everything is nothing—or maybe something—oh I ached for it to be!

Your coffee is a black hole, but with milk in it it's a milky hole.

Somewhere someone is being killed, but nothing is anything, right, so you don't have to worry about that, right, you don't have to care. But you *want* to worry, you *want* to care. You want to feel what you're not feeling.

Pills and the bottle won't help—you know they won't, you've seen they won't—but what will?

There's nothing but the toast and butter, books and grades, and your would-be career—all shells of your life, now in a pile rotting.

That's how, in retrospect, I'd say it was. But back then I'd have told you only that I was in a funk, a bit of a fog.

22.

And into this fog came a letter. Yes, again a letter! But now of a different kind.

It was from Fr. Bates, a friendly note prompted by an acquaintance he'd made. At a conference on Cardinal Neman he'd met Princeton's Catholic chaplain, Fr. Charles Weiser. "He's a good man," he said. "You should look him up."

I had seen Fr. Bates only twice since we'd left Indiana in 1977. He'd visited us in Seattle once and I'd stopped to see him on my way to Princeton. The latter visit had given me a better sense of him. I learned we shared a love of history. We discussed when the "modern" age began, and he unfolded a timeline of world history that later gave me the idea for my own study-aid at Princeton. He asked about the family, my high school years, and my hopes for the future. He told me, too, about Newman: his conversion to Catholicism and facility as a writer. Then Fr. Bates wished me well and sent me off with some spending money.

Seeing the letter reminded me of something he'd said at that time: "For me," he said, "the strongest argument for God's existence is the logic of desire. For every longing there is an answer. Just look at your daily life. For thirst there is water. For hunger, food. For loneliness, friendship. Why then would there not be an answer for the deepest, most important longing within us, for the fullness of life itself—for peace and goodness and happiness?"

23.

When the mass was over, I approached the white-haired priest. "Are you Fr. Weisen?"

"Weiser," he said, "like Budweiser."

We agreed to meet on Tuesday at the Aquinas Institute. "Do you know where it is?

It turned out I didn't. When I rang the bell at St. Paul's, the pastor redirected me. He called Fr. Weiser to say I'd be late.

"I don't know exactly why I'm here. I guess I've got some questions. I've been doing a lot thinking and having a hard time. I'm stuck."

Though I said I had questions, it was mostly Fr. Weiser who did the asking. I babbled on and on.

Occasionally he asked for clarification, or said one of my words back to me. "Perfect" was one.

At the end I said, "I'd like to learn more about the Church."

He said, "I suggest you hang around it." Then he stood and selected a book. "You may find this helpful."

It was called *A New Catechism*.

24.

When I stepped outside that night I looked up to find the sky cold and vast and full of stars. It had never looked so big and open. It was the damnedest thing. When I'd gone in I'd felt as though the whole cosmos was clamped down tight on my head, like a metal helmet. But now it was all open again. I felt myself suddenly free.

25.

That conversation laid the foundation for my belief in confession. I hadn't made a by-the-book, sacramental confession, but I had poured out my soul and walked away feeling liberated.

That night changed my life. Every day since has been lived in the light of it. I'd been in the pit and somehow God had pulled me out. He'd done for me what I couldn't do for myself.

I don't know what more to say about it. God went from being a question to a presence.

26.

Did this really happen? In the days that followed I shook my head in amazement. I felt a touch of giddiness, but mostly deeply serene gratitude for my newfound freedom.

Fr. Weiser had said, "Hang around the church." What did that mean?

I gathered he was recommending attending mass, but I sensed he was also suggesting more generally that I get a feel for the church—its people and practices.

So I did. I started going to mass.

One afternoon, out of the blue, I felt a sudden need to be in the chapel. I sprinted across campus, and stood heaving, staring at the cross in the transept. I had the whole place to myself. I sat down in the middle of it and soaked it all in. Then I raised my eyes to heaven. *Is anybody there?*

I wondered if I were now officially crazy, speaking to a God I didn't believe in.

But I didn't feel crazy. I heard no answer, but I felt my words had landed. I'd been heard.

So this is prayer.

I've been praying ever since.

I might have worried the sky would soon close again or that I would find myself back in the pit. But I didn't. Somehow I knew it wasn't going to happen. I've never lost that feeling of freedom and of God's presence.

27.

My best learnings at Princeton happened outside the classroom. The catechism Fr. Weiser gave me proved very helpful. In later years, when I found myself living and working in the Netherlands, I would take it as a sign that he'd given me the famous (if initially controversial) *Dutch Catechism*. What I liked about it was that it began with the very questions I was wrestling with: *Is there any point to life? Why do people believe in God? What does faith involve?*

Significantly, too, it provided me with a bridge to the Bible. For as a budding English major, I wasn't sure what to make of it. A friend's mom had said, "You should read the Bible, even if only because it's so often referred to in literature." But I never had. Now I turned the Bible over in my hands. It was like a glowing rock I'd dug up in Egypt. What power did it hold? I remembered how Dad's blue Bible had been one of the few possessions that had made the cut and traveled with us to Arizona, back in '73.

I started with Matthew's Gospel. Jesus came straight at me: "One does not live by bread alone, but by every word that comes forth from the mouth of God." And: "If the light in you is darkness, how great will the darkness be." Most challenging of all in my first go-around were his words "Stop judging, that you may not be judged." I thought of all the times, back in the student center at P.A. High, when I'd casually decided whether passersby measured up in the ways they spoke, acted, and dressed. I never shared negative views of people to their face, of course (which was what made me a "nice person"), but I didn't hesitate to share it with my friends. Flipping back through my journal of that year, I noted I'd dismissed some kids as "scums." But here was Jesus with a higher standard. He knew what people had in their hearts, I did not. Judgment was for God, not for me.

I kept the Bible open on my desk. During breaks in my studies I'd read the Psalms. What an eye-opener! Who knew prayer was like this? I'd thought it was all about kowtowing to God and asking Him to give you stuff and make you a good boy. But now I saw you could also have it out with God. The Psalms were full of agony and doubt and pleading. Yes, there was lots of praise and thanks to God, but I saw too you can be perfectly frank with Him, and I discovered that faith in its essence is a relationship of trust. So I let God have it with my "Bad News." I told Him we were barely scraping by down here and He was dropping the ball on the world. I pointed out my parents' struggles and my sister's and my own, and how so many of us down here were in pain.

28.

That summer in Port Angeles, Sung asked, "What happened?"

I said, "It came down to a conflict between my head and my heart. My head said love is meaningless, but my heart said it's right to love. I knew my heart was right, so I questioned my thinking."

It took him and Jack some getting used to, me going to church and piously watching my words. But I wasn't entirely on the straight and narrow. In fact, I almost missed my first communion. What almost made me miss it was a dance the night before. We three parked to drink before the dance and then bounded into the gym like a trio of frisky rabbits. Two hours later I wasn't sober enough to drive.

"Boys, we're going to have to walk." We trudged up the hill to Mom and Dad's, no big deal. We were glad for the fresh air. We passed out on mattresses in the electric heat of my bedroom.

In the morning I woke to a helluva hangover. I saw I had twenty minutes to get to mass. Then it hit me: I didn't have a car! In a panic I called the Turners'. They were back in P.A. now. "Is anyone by chance heading down the hill?"

As it happened—and here is your proof of providence—Dr. Turner was leaving for the clinic in five minutes. I covered my stench with a jacket and tie, and entered the church just in time.

29.

And so in my four years there I found a very different Princeton from the one I expected to find. This was driven home during a weekday mass in the chapel. The psalm said, "Put not your trust in princes, in man, in whom there is no salvation."

I'd learned my lesson. Now I was trusting in the Prince of Peace.

Louvain

1

"Is that the kind of priest you want to be?"

I hadn't seen the question coming and wondered why Fr. Meyer asked it. But yes, Fr. Michael, our parochial vicar in Port Angeles—the sandy-haired, pale-blue-eyed former linebacker from San Diego—was the first one I thought of when I imagined myself a priest. The pastor called him "the golden boy." He'd be at the football games on Friday and drag the youth to the coast on Saturday. On Sunday he nailed the homily: five minutes, a strong image, no wasted words, no torturing you with his own lack of clarity.

Maybe Fr. Meyer thought he was too conservative.

Fr. Michael had prepared me for my first communion and he'd heard my first confession. But there were lots of priests who set me an example. Fr. Robert Imbelli was another. He was a systematic theologian who'd shown me the richness of the Catholic tradition. He'd been at Princeton when I was there and had given me wise guidance in spiritual direction. Thomas Merton, no longer living but whose writings I admired, was another. And Fr. Bruce Ritter, who ran a shelter for homeless youth in New York. I'd thought of volunteering at Fr. Ritter's Covenant House. But after graduation I went back to Seattle instead.

2.

A friend's dad thought priesthood would be "wasting my life." But I saw it as the opposite, as the very best thing I could do with my life: offering it up to God in service of my neighbor. God had radically intervened to save me. It only seemed fitting to give radical witness to that.

People said, "Celibacy, celibacy . . ." as if that were all there was to priesthood. But if celibacy was for me the primary obstacle to priesthood, it was also part of the attraction. Therein lay the sacrifice: I didn't want to do something easy with my life, I wanted to do something hard.

Celibacy, moreover, in a sex-obsessed world, made people sit up and take notice. It was countercultural. It gave pause.

Practically speaking, I believed making this choice would free me up to serve people in ways I couldn't do otherwise. By giving up a family of my own, I could be available to those who had no family. During college I'd spent my summers working in summer camps where I'd seen kids who were without a father. Maybe I could be a kind of surrogate father. More importantly, maybe I could help people see and trust our Father in heaven.

3.

The Seattle Archdiocese put me through the wringer, of course. And rightly so! They didn't know me at all when I wrote, and would-be seminarians typically have their issues. They interviewed me and gave me a battery of tests. They sent me to one psychologist and then another. Finally they put me in a program called Channel. Fr. Meyer (one more psychologist!) was assigned to oversee my progress. If all went well I would enter a seminary the following fall.

4.

Channel was great for me. It was a one-to-two-year hothouse experience for people just out of college. It was designed to prepare them for ministry, teaching, or social service. Twenty of us spent the summer in formation and then the rest of the year, under supervision, in jobs in our chosen field. Especially helpful to me were the exercises in self-awareness we partook of in the summer months. We were taught to look closely at our personal history in order to identify potential strengths and weaknesses in our future ministry. For the first time in my life I spoke openly with others about my family history.

Happily, this coincided with Mom and Dad's own excavation of the past. While I was still at Princeton, Dad had gotten to know a man in Port Angeles, Bruce Webster, who worked with Vietnam veterans. Bruce sought out men who'd been traumatized by the war and put them in touch with one another and with resources available for their support. Bruce sometimes went deep into the forest to find these men. At that time we were only just starting to hear about post-traumatic stress disorder (PTSD). Bruce was a big help to Dad and my mom, and indirectly to me and my sister. Though I spoke with him only once in my life, I owe him an eternal debt of gratitude. I have the highest admiration for the patience, guts, and love he showed.

5.

My jobs that year were in a parish and in a food bank. Together with four other Channelites, I lived in a dicey neighborhood in the Central District. My big blue boat—a Caprice Classic donated by a parishioner—ferried me from there (where the food bank was) to the rich suburb where I served as a youth minister.

It was a good year. I liked my housemates and got to see Sung (who was now vice-president of the student body at the University of Washington) on the weekends. Though my love of women tormented me, I focused on my "calling." In the spring life took an exciting turn when Fr. Meyer raised the possibility of me studying in Europe the following year, at the Catholic University of Louvain. I was all for that! I'd never been to Europe.

But then I got thrown for a loop. One of the last hurdles before the decision on seminary was an interview with another psychologist, this time, surprisingly, an attractive woman religious.

We talked about my personal history and motivation, and then she pressed me on my prior romantic involvements. "Tell me more about your relationships with women," she said. "I'm hearing a lot of sighing."

By that time I'd needed to pee for quite some time. I asked to be excused. At the urinal I thought, *This looks bad.*

When we finished she said, "Do you need more time? Do you want another year to think about it?"

The question filled me with panic.

Fr. Meyer asked, "How did it go?"

"Not so good, I think."

He got a concerned look.

My intuition was proven correct. Fr. Jaeger, the director of seminarians, said I had two options. If I wanted to study in Washington, D.C., at the Catholic University of America, I could have the green light immediately. They had a psychologist in place who would be available to work with me. But if I wanted to go to Louvain, I would first need to see a psychologist for six weeks, and then they would decide.

Boy was I pissed! I mean, sure, I had my issues. Giving up on sex and marriage was difficult. But wasn't it *supposed to be difficult*? Wasn't that the whole point, that celibacy was a *sacrifice*?

And who was this woman to judge me and kill my plans? She'd only just met me. I'd spent the last three years preparing myself for seminary. Couldn't I at least try? How was I ever to know unless I tried?

What was I supposed to say to people now? *No, still don't know about seminary. The diocese needs to decide if I'm crazy first.*

It was humiliating and it sent me into a tailspin. But I hardly dared speak of it. It was too embarrassing.

6.

The worst of it was, after sucking it up and meeting with the psychologist and finally getting my yes for Louvain, I *still* blew it. While unwinding with some friends, I downed one margarita too many and spent the wee hours with a lovely woman who was sympathetic to my situation. Hells bells! as Dad would say. Hopeless. While driving her home the next morning, I saw a sticker on the car ahead: "It's a dog-eat-dog world and I'm wearing Milkbone underwear."

I drove to Madison Park, where I sat dazed and depressed, staring out at the lake. This hadn't been a hedonistic, meaningless thing. This was a great girl who I liked a lot. Under other circumstances I would have been delighted to have tangled with her. But now I was supposed to be embracing my calling (if that's what it was), not opening the door to some new romantic involvement. *Crap, look at this day, freaking perfect, crystal-clear, just mocking me.*

Seeing my Princeton sweatshirt, a fellow alumnus (who I did not know) stopped to chat. "Did you just graduate?"

I was in no mood to reminisce about Old Nassau. Why was I such a screw-up? St. Paul was right: I do what I don't want to do, and don't do what I do. Shooby-dooby-doo. Friggin' A.

7.

This misadventure I kept it to myself. Well, I did tell Sung. And his girlfriend took one look at my face and guessed it right away. But I sure didn't say anything about it to Fr. Meyer. They had enough reason to doubt me already. Fr. Meyer had said he deemed me a "high-risk seminarian."

Then came another blow, from another direction. I heard it on the radio on my way to work. Fr. Paul, the priest who'd succeeded Fr. Michael in Port Angeles, had been arrested on charges of child molestation. At the staff meeting that morning, I broke down in tears.

I knew Fr. Paul. Not well, but I knew him. He'd given me a ride from Seattle to P.A. once, and he'd joined Mom and Dad and me for dinner. (Since my conversion they'd started going to church again themselves.) I liked him. He didn't have the easy way with people that Fr. Michael had, but he was smart, he had a good look about him. He was friendly and serious.

Now he was in jail.

8.

What a relief it was in July to pack all my worldly goods and head for Beaver Lake—to Camp Cabrini in the foothills of the Cascades. I'd worked there before as a counselor and now would serve as chaplain. I saw it all before me—the trees, the dining hall, the soccer field. I perked up as I drove. Back in the open air! "Come not here if you have already spent the best of yourself," Walt Whitman had said. What a theologian that man was! He dared to go forth and truly live. Didn't Christ talk about life in abundance?

I stepped out and smelled the fresh-cut grass. Big Paul Denini sat strumming "Sugar Magnolia" on his guitar. He had a Paul Bunyan thing going that summer. We all had our characters, our roles we (wittingly or not) played for the kids. His sister Susan was like a mom to us.

Before campfire came evening reflection, down by the lake. Jeff, the director, said, "Pick a spot in the distance, something to focus on. We'll come down here every evening. Maybe it will change, maybe you will change."

Jeff was scrappy and had a sandpaper voice. He taught P.E. and coached wrestling at O'Dea High School. He read to us from *On the Loose* (great book!) and sang "Comes a Time."

My spot was a young tree, rising from a floating dock.

After campfire came the prayer. That was my job.

9.

That summer put me back together. We rose, prayed, and raised the flag. We ate pancakes, hiked, and played three-ball soccer. We rowed and swam. During chaplain's hour I had the kids carry rocks (their burdens) and throw them away. I proclaimed the Good News from the top of a shed, and when Elly, the littlest camper, captured the flag and brought it across the line I saw in it a sign of God's salvation: "A little child shall lead them."

Those kids were alive and I came alive too.

A man-size cross stood on the porch of my cabin. In my free time I liked to sit there and read. Kids walked by. "Hey, Chap, we're coming to see you today." One afternoon Jeff stopped by. He sat on the step. "Seminary, huh?"

"Yes, hard to believe."

"You can't join us on the overnight?"

"No, I tried to get out of it, but Fr. Jaeger says the meeting is mandatory."

"That's all right. He always was a hard-ass. I was on staff when he was director. How long have you been thinking about seminary?"

"Three years."

"A good priest can really make a difference." He looked up through the trees. "I wish I had a plan. Sometimes I don't know what the hell I'm doing."

It surprised me. He was ten years older, had a good job, was directing this camp. From what I saw, he had it all figured out. But I knew things could look better on the outside than they felt on the inside.

10.

On the last day we put the kids on the bus and cleaned up the camp. I took a picture of my little tree and then left for P.A., to spend time with Mom and Dad before leaving for seminary.

It was good to be back home, to see them and some old friends. I laughed when Dad put on Pink Floyd on the way to mass.

Hearing I was in town, Dr. Turner called. He and Suzanne and Shelley were going to camp at Boulder Lake. Did I want to come along? I did!

The hike up took four hours. We picked huckleberries and claimed Dr. Turner's favorite spot, an outcropping under hemlock, right by the water. It was hot, but he was glad to see a patch of snow. He wanted to test the warmth of his new sleeping bag. We put up the tents and swam. Shelley batted away gnats. I sat on a rock and read Hopkins—poems and journal entries.

Suzanne asked me about seminary. She, like so many others, thought celibacy was a dumb requirement: priests ought to be able to marry. She'd been raised in the Lutheran church, but now at

Stanford was active in an evangelical group. I gathered from our conversation that she was pretty strict on the matter of premarital involvements. Not only was premarital sex out of the question, so was making-out. I had to laugh. She was stricter than I (supposedly) was. *Kissing was a slippery slope!* Well, maybe it was.

We cast for fish, but what we'd brought with us was what was for dinner. The wood smoke smelled exceedingly fine. I stared into the fire's embers. Dr. Turner played "Moon River" on the harmonica. I slept peacefully in my tent.

In the morning we hiked back down. We lowered the top of their VW for the drive home. It was too noisy to talk.

11.

While still on the Peninsula, I drove out to see Fr. Michael. He was stationed on the coast now, at Our Lady of Good Help. The glowing reports on his work on Port Angeles had won him an assignment at the cathedral in Seattle, but Fr. Michael hadn't liked being in the city. He'd stayed only two years. Hoquiam was a better fit. It was smaller and, even better, full of birds. He loved to watch them. "Come on," he said, "I'll show you."

I thought we'd be sitting in a blind somewhere, but we got in his truck and covered fifty miles. Every so often he pulled over to point out a heron or pelican or common murre. "Look," he said, "a flicker." We leaned into the windshield. It flashed red as it rose.

Fr. Michael had the kind of rectory I would want. Simple, orderly, with lots of books and windows. His empty mug sat on the end table where he prayed his morning office.

"Do the seminarians there wear clerics?" he asked. "Let me know when you need them. I'll buy you your first set."

12.

When Mom and Dad drove me to the airport, it reminded me of the olden days. They'd traded in the Wagoneer for a '56 Ford Fairlane. Normally this car gave them no trouble, but now, twenty miles from the airport, it started sputtering. Dad kept to the right, driving thirty and swearing all the way. "I guess God doesn't want Tim to go to the seminary!"

But I guess God did, because we made it. Dad pulled over to the curb at Sea-Tac. Mom got out to give me a hug. "You'll understand if we don't come in."

When I boarded that Sabena flight to Brussels I had two books with me: *Don Quixote* and *The Right Stuff*. Yeager, the Air Force test pilot—faster than the speed of sound, flying by the seat of his pants! I'd loved Sam Shepard in the film and now I found the same free-wheeling quality in Tom Wolfe's writing. That was how priesthood was going to be: Tim the ace rocketing over the desert!

13.

The Catholic University of Louvain—or Leuven, in Dutch—was founded in 1425. The American College seminary, where I lived, was a small institution, independent of the university but associated with it. It had been established in 1857 to train European missionaries for service in North America, but in my time seminarians from the United States and other parts of the world came to the College to take advantage of the university's renowned faculties of philosophy and theology. Classes were offered in English as well as in Dutch. Priests and seminarians in the US commonly saw the American College as the progressive counterpart to the North American College in Rome. If you thought God might be calling you to become a bishop, you had a better shot at becoming one in the more "orthodox" seminary in Rome than you did in Leuven, which lived (and sometimes died) by the historical-critical method.

Two seminarians in street clothes met me at the airport. Zaventem was not noticeably different from any other airport I'd been in, apart from the signs in Dutch and French. Nor did the highway between Brussels and Leuven show me the European Magic Kingdom I expected. But Leuven itself was in line with what I'd envisioned. Tall houses of stone rose from narrow sidewalks. Much of the architecture was centuries old, the stunning centerpiece being the town hall, with its lacelike stone, Gothic arches, turrets, and Biblical scenes.

On my first walk through town I was grateful to have that building and the adjacent St. Peter's church as reference points, because I was now off the American grid. The streets here did not run parallel and perpendicular, but radiated out as spokes from the church to the surrounding "ring," with winding side streets connecting the spokes. Heightening my disorientation was my inability to pronounce the words I saw on the signs. The broad boulevard running from the train station into the middle of town was called the *Bondgenotenlaan*. Later I learned that meant "Lane of the Allies." It honored the allied troops who had liberated the city at the end of World War II. As in the woods, I made note of markers at every turn, looking back in order to recognize the way home.

14.

The seminary rector, Fr. Tom Ivory, rounded the corner as I waited for the elevator. He welcomed me and suggested I rest before dinner. After a nap I wandered the halls. Pinned to the bulletin board, I found a photocopy of an article from the *National Catholic Reporter*. The editor had passed through Leuven in the spring. He'd been reassured, he wrote, by his conversations with the seminarians there, who'd struck him as even-keel and not too clerical or unworldly. The rector, he said, looked like Cary Grant in his later years.

In the lounge I met Paul, another first-year guy. He'd arrived a few days before from California. Since I'd missed lunch, we walked down the narrow street behind the seminary to a pub frequented by the "brothers." He ordered us each a pint and a *croque monsieur*. Paul said he was glad to move on from his old seminary. There he'd been hassled by some fellow seminarians—gay guys who joked around in a way he found totally irritating. This raised a question that had been in the back of my mind for some time: How would homosexuality factor into my seminary experience?

It had already become clear to me that a significant portion of the seminarians and priests I'd met over the last three years were gay. Certainly not all, but enough for me to notice. Being somewhat homophobic, I hoped to avoid the matter altogether. "How is that here?" I asked.

Paul said the guys he'd met so far were mature and serious. "I don't care if they're gay," he said, "but I hope they know how to deal with their sexuality responsibly."

Back in high school, the word "fag" got tossed around casually. At the time, though, it had never occurred to me that anyone I knew actually *was* gay, not even guys who had stereotypically "effeminate" mannerisms. By the time I graduated from Princeton, though, I had more realistic view, and my Channel year really opened my eyes. There, a number of people—men and women—spoke candidly of their (homo)sexuality. These people—just as full of faith and as intent on serving as I was—shared how difficult it had been, hiding this crucial aspect of themselves for fear of condemnation.

I wasn't sure what to make of it all. I knew the Bible had verses censuring homosexual acts, and the Congregation for the Doctrine of the Faith had recently released a document calling such acts "intrinsically disordered." That statement had gotten a lot of attention, and as it happened my own Archbishop, Raymond Hunthausen, was in hot water with the Vatican for, among other things, having allowed a group of openly gay Catholics—affiliated under the name Dignity—to gather for a weekly Mass in the cathedral.

On two points I'd made up my mind. Every gay person I'd spoken to saw his or her sexuality as just the way they were. Many had actively tried to ignore or overcome their orientation—since the price of being openly gay in society was so high—but none had succeeded. So I didn't believe in conversion therapy. Nor was I inclined to hound people about their sex life in general. At Princeton there'd been a big stink, shortly after my time, about a priest who'd done just that.

15.

There were seven in my year: Arnie, from Canada, and Phu, Tom B., Christian, Michael, Paul, and me, all from the US. We spent the first week learning Dutch. Belgians in the northern part of the country (in Flanders, where we were) spoke Dutch (Flemish), while those in the South (in Wallonia) spoke French. I knew I'd be studying a lot of languages in the years ahead. Though our courses would be in English, we would also need to learn Latin, Greek, and Hebrew. I wasn't too keen on that, frankly, but I *was* motivated to learn Dutch because I wanted to be able to communicate with people in town and not just with those studying theology.

During the week, Fr. Ivory checked on us individually. He knocked on my door. "Are you settling in all right? How's it going?"

I invited him in. I said I was enjoying it. I opened up. I told him I'd had a rough spring and that celibacy was still a struggle, but I was glad to be here.

He listened attentively and thanked me. "They say celibacy is a gift, but it's not an easy gift."

In my first journal entries in the seminary I piously called him "Father Rector," but I soon bagged that and began calling him Tom, like everyone else did. Some weeks later, in a homily, he told us about his youth—about how his dad had lost his job at General Motors because of a heart condition and his mom then went to work selling greeting cards and washing windows. When it came time for high school, his pastor chipped in half the tuition and his mom worked on Saturdays to pay the rest. Later he learned his parents were embarrassed his only nice clothes were an old suit of his dad's.

16.

When Tom was a student in Leuven, the seminarians wore a cassock and *saturno*, the brim of which they rolled up to look like a cowboy hat. We, however, were not required to wear clerics, nor did the priests on staff or Belgian priests in town wear them. They wore only a cross pin on the lapel. This disappointed me. I thought if you were going to be a priest you should look like one.

Our day began in the chapel. Classes were not in "the house" but at the Maria Theresia College down the street. We had two-hour lectures. During the break we adjourned to the drafty hall, where you could buy coffee and warm your butt by the radiator. Sometimes we ran into Flemish students, a mix of seminarians, priests, and laypersons (men and women). Mass was at 5:00 p.m., back at the chapel. That was a good time for it. The twilight closed in in a comforting way. My favorite window showed Christ with a sword and a lily. He looked at me and I looked at him.

17.

After dinner guys would study. Or not. Sometimes we went out for a beer, one of the abbey beers Belgium is famous for. In the beginning we went as a group, but I quickly tired of that. At first it was nice to have the company, but after a while it seemed we were always talking about the same old stuff—about people's idiosyncrasies and ecclesiastical minutiae. I couldn't get too worked up about the finer points of liturgical style or a priest who'd spent $10,000 on a chalice. Being in a group kept the conversation mostly superficial.

Knowing I was interested in meeting people outside the house, an upperclassman from Seattle, Dennis, invited me to the university parish. "They have a mass for students on Wednesday, with a simple meal afterwards." There I met three people who became friends: two German students, and a Belgian girl named Noëmi. Noëmi had just spent a year studying in Steubenville, Ohio. She looked very Flemish. She was straight out of a painting by Van Eyck.

18.

Looking up to Jesus, I kept wondering, *What now?* I wanted some specific, concrete guidance.

Following him was a funny business. I didn't actually see or hear him (though mystics sometimes did). The first step in my approach to him had been learning to believe in God in general. I'd had to ask myself, Could I reasonably do such a thing? The great thing about Princeton was that everyone there was intelligent, and many were believers. So clearly you could be a rational person and still believe in God. People speak of a "leap of faith" as if embracing faith means abandoning reason. But whenever I spoke with people about their faith they gave me their reasons for believing. Typically it was because they'd had a personal experience of God, as I had. They had in some sense *met* God. Faith was not so much believing *that* God was there, but letting God *into* your life. The "leap" was not of the head, but of the heart: it was an act of trust. You learned to trust God in a relationship.

The second step, I'd discovered, was getting acquainted with Jesus himself. I'd known of him from the culture at large (from references in films, books, songs), but after my conversion I got to know him through the Bible, the mass, prayer, and fellow believers. Christ instructed and challenged me by all of these means. He didn't say things directly. Instead some of his words or an image of him would stand out and resonate strongly. I would know it was something he wanted me to hear and reflect on. Such as: "Love one another as I have loved you." When I heard that, shortly before my confirmation, I thought: *That's a different way of loving than what I've known.*

But how do you do that exactly, love in Christ's way? Now instead of being in a parish or food bank, where opportunities to do that seemed readily available, I was in a place where my primary task was to study. It made me antsy.

19.

Heightening my restlessness were my courses at the university. Fr. Michael had said, "Study for the glory of God," but at the moment I barely had to study at all. This was a very different system from the one I'd known. At Princeton, beyond attending lectures, we were also expected to go to precepts, read everything on the syllabus, write papers, and take a midterm and three-hour final. The essay-final synthesized all you'd learned. It was a shock then in Leuven—a not unpleasant shock at first—to see how little we had to do. Yes, there were lectures, but for most we had printed transcripts available. And while we did have to take an exam in each course, that was a short oral exam at the end of the school year. Our grades were based entirely on those brief conversations in the spring.

I heard from upperclassmen that all we were expected to do in the exam was say back to the professor exactly what he'd said to us. This struck me as a narrow way to train minds. But I certainly didn't miss writing papers and taking midterms. Thus did I, along with my classmates, sit for four to six hours a day listening to a professor read to us from the very text we had before us. Since I could read in a quarter of the time he or she could speak, I typically ignored the sound and wrote letters.

20.

The psychologist who worked with me in Leuven was named Maridel. Occasionally on my way in I ran into a brother on his way out. I wanted to ask, "What are you in for?"

Maridel had just finished her doctorate in psychology. Being Catholic herself, she came to mass at the seminary.

When I first sat down in her office, she said, "So tell me about yourself."

I told her I was actually quite tired of focusing on myself. "Shouldn't I be turning to something more important by now, like God and my neighbor?"

"Do you know yourself well enough? Can you do that freely?"

"I don't know, but all the self-reflection bogs me down. It's like a trap."

"How long have you felt this way?"

Oh God, I thought, *here we go*.

I trusted Maridel from the start. In contrast with my experience in Seattle, I did not feel she was first and foremost a gatekeeper for the Archdiocese. Yes, she would report back to them, but primarily she was there for me.

I told her my parents were getting counseling as well. "They're filing a claim with the V.A."

Bruce Webster was helping with that. It was a disability claim with the Veterans Administration. For the first time, Dad had started opening up about his time in Vietnam. During my last visit he'd told me about the rocket that hit his track, killing the friend who rode next to him, and about the fear and violence he still re-lived on a daily basis. What to me was a plate of risotto was to him that friend's brains.

I was glad to read the report Mom and Dad filed with the V.A. It recounted their experience since the war and gave me new perspective on our family history. Mom said the first time she'd noticed a difference after the war was when we drove from Indiana to Fort Ord. After a stop at a drive-in, Mom misread the map and Dad freaked out, fearing they were lost in a bad part of the Bay Area. He'd snapped at Mom and thrown his burger out the window.

I didn't remember it, but I could totally see it.

21.

I kept Sung posted on the latest developments at the seminary, bragging about the lavish banquet we'd had to kick off the year (drinks in the rector's garden, a five-course meal, cigars, liqueurs) and all the traveling I was doing. (I was just back from Vienna and right after Christmas my class would go to Rome.) Sung compli-mented me on my placement. He was drinking coffee at the Last Exit and reading Hemingway. He couldn't wait to come over. We planned to travel together that summer.

22.

On December 26 my classmates and I boarded a train to Rome. It was good to be on the move. Christmas had been depressing. For the first time in my life, I spent it away from family, and no cards had arrived before the holiday.

St. Peter's, the Sistine Chapel, a private mass with the pope—
you'd think it would be dazzling. It was, but it wasn't. It was interesting, for sure. I'd first read about Pope John Paul II when I was in
high school. *Time* had said he was brilliant (he spoke half a dozen
languages), and young for a pope. He was athletic, too—a hiker
and a skier. Now, having faced down the Communist regime in
Poland, he was spearheading revival (or retrenchment, depending
on your view) in the Church. What more famous person in the
world could I meet? Here was the leader of the Church, the Vicar
of Christ.

He shook our hands and gave us each a rosary. Then we gathered around him for the photo. I thought, "Wow, I'm looking at the
back of the pope's ear." But I felt nothing more uplifting than that.

The brothers and I stayed at the North American College. It
was a massive place, with a soccer field and fifty orange trees (one
for each state). I liked the pasta, but was glad I wasn't studying
there. It sat on a hill and was way more isolated than our place was.
I'd go nuts there.

23.

Back in Leuven, Sr. Marguerite, who tended the front door, had a
tip for me. Hearing me fret about our luxurious confinement, she
suggested I go to Poverello, a local soup kitchen. They were looking for volunteers.

When I visited, the woman in charge said, "Great! When are
you available?" She put me to work cutting onions.

Seeing my tears, she laughed. "That's all right. We'll put you
behind the bar."

Later I'd see people from Poverello at Stuc, a café I discovered
around the same time. People like "the Red One." "That's what they
call me," he said, and I could imagine. He was burly, with red hair
and a red beard.

Like Poverello, Stuc was also a good place to go to escape the
enclosure of the seminary. Stuc stood for "student café," but I noted it was also a homonym of the Dutch word *stuk*, which means

broken. I started going there whenever I had an hour free, to drink a *koffie verkeerd* and write in my journal.

24.

The theology department sometimes let us take an exam or two halfway through the year, so I had my first ones in January. They went fine but the exam period gave me pause. For while it was fun to boast of taking Greek and Hebrew, it wasn't fun having to learn first the characters and then the words and grammar. To what end? When would I use it in the parish? I didn't mean to be a scholar or someone climbing the ranks of the hierarchy (who would need the proper degrees). I was tired of school and wasn't inclined to pave the way for a future job in the chancery. I dreaded the thought of managing stuff. I was having a tough enough time managing myself.

Moreover, I didn't *have* to take Greek and Hebrew. If I transitioned from the canonical-degree track (which led to the ecclesiastical STB and STL degrees) to the secular track that led to the BA and MA in religious studies, I wouldn't need to take the languages. In addition I would be done in four years instead of five, which would put me in the parish a year earlier.

It didn't require much thought. I decided to switch.

But the rector didn't see it my way, nor did the archdiocese. They spoke of "developing my God-given abilities" and "not limiting my options," adding the assurance that the language courses would be over soon enough. Tom told me to pray about it and discuss it with my spiritual director.

25.

I couldn't really afford magazines, but when I saw Sam Shepard on the cover of *Esquire*, I couldn't resist. Man, what a cool guy: a writer *and* a cowboy *and* a movie star *and* married to Jessica Lange. But also trying to ditch it all and disappear, picking up his mail at a hardware store. He said his early days in New York were "an astounding time 'cause it was non-stop blood-and-guts work.

It was just wonderful to be an artist, not to sit around in your loft somewhere thinking about it."

Shit yes! I totally got it, not least his flippy relationship with his dad. I loved how he wrote, and I noticed my own writing had gotten looser. Maybe the scratchings in my journal were the seeds of poetry (or perhaps just the elliptical musings of a crazy man).

I quoted Shepard to the brothers: "I'd rather rope steers / Than talk politics with you."

26.

Was I growing in holiness? I noted the grooves worn in the steps by all those who'd gone before. Had their time in the seminary made them holy? What even did that mean, holy? The word suggested something sensual, like the sound of an angel choir.

Lord, can't You ever just take charge? How about some guidance?

I imagined what he'd say: *You already have what you need.*

27.

How much loneliness is too much? A friend wrote: "Do you feel it's the human condition to be lonely? God, how many times have I heard that? We have such intricate minds, are capable of such astounding things in everyday life. Then why isn't it good enough to be alone with ourselves? I can't understand this damn viper of loneliness. I feel for you greatly."

The Jesus of the window looked lonely. Surely he must have been when he was in the desert, and in the garden, and on the cross.

28.

In December Noëmi had invited me to Antwerp, to decorate the Christmas tree with her and her family. They lived in an art nouveau house in Berchem. She had a brother my age, a sister a year or two younger, and a brother and sister in grade school. When her equally beautiful sister reached to hang an ornament, I thought: "I'm falling for two girls at once."

Her youngest sister played the violin. At dinner they all laughed at my inability to roll my "R." (I hadn't been able to do it in Spanish either.)

I was just glad to be taken in.

29.

When I recounted my visit to Maridel, she said, "Tim, you are hopelessly heterosexual. It's refreshing!"

From this I gathered it made me exceptional, but what did I know? We didn't speak openly of sexuality in the seminary. A implicit don't-ask-don't-tell policy applied.

To a degree I understood and welcomed the silence. I didn't want to get into those discussions either. Later in life, though, I would feel a deep sadness about this. After a priest friend died, I realized we'd never had the candid conversation I'd always hoped we'd have. I sensed he struggled with his sexual identity—suffered in a Church that didn't want him to be who he really was—and on more than one occasion I tried to open the door to a conversation about this. But he never walked through that door. Maybe I sent off the wrong vibe. I hope not.

Indeed, it's a shame we of the Church don't address these matters directly. Especially since sexual longing and the desire for God intermingle. Aren't both passionate cries for completion? Weren't the Beatles and Dylan when they said, "I want you so bad" saying exactly what Augustine was saying in *The Confessions*, and with the same energy? I've always loved how Augustine's God-talk is suffused with desire ("I will grasp you. Do not hide your face from me . . . Let me see your face lest I die"), even when his very subject is *transcending* desire ("Oh, that I might rest in you. Oh, that you would enter my heart so as to overwhelm it"). Then again, how could there *not* be affinity between sexual and spiritual desire, given that God is the source and destination of all that exists? Surely then every desire is to some extent a reflection of and participation in our ultimate desire for God?

Fr. Imbelli, in one of our early conversations, introduced me to St. Irenaeus's concept of recapitulation—that creation flows from Christ and comes to summation in him. He turns all things to the good. So even our screw-ups and selfish desires have a role in God's ultimate big picture. Someday, God willing, we'll see how this all fits together. I can't wait for that.

30.

My spiritual director signed off on the program change. I could breathe more easily. I no longer needed to study Greek and Hebrew.

When I explained my reasons for making the switch, the brothers in my year listened sympathetically but none followed suit. With Paul, I understood the lack of interest. He was smart and driven. To get the canonical degrees and spend that extra year in Leuven made sense for him. Later he completed a doctorate and served as director of worship for the Diocese of Oakland. He oversaw construction of their beautiful Cathedral of Light. But most guys seemed better suited to parish work. So why not keep it simple?

In theory, camaraderie with the brothers should have been the antidote for my loneliness. There was ample opportunity to get to know them and the priests in the house. To a degree, it worked that way. I could relate to Mike next door and Tom B. two doors down. Both were laid back and easy to talk to. I also liked Matua, an upperclassman from Uganda. When he spoke of losing family members in the civil war in Uganda it reminded us all that church service didn't reduce to internal, parochial concerns. Dave and Al, along with Paul, joined me in a "growth group" (mutual support group). And the priests Terry, Pat, and Dick were all good guys. And Tom Ivory, of course, who had become a friend, though it seemed some viewed our friendship with misgiving. I brushed that aside. Tom was always looking for someone to play racquetball. The fact that others didn't take him up on it wasn't my problem. In Rome he and I had traveled to Naples together to see a friend of his, a Navy chaplain. It was fun.

So there was opportunity enough to connect with guys, but it never quite met my need. For me it was just easier to open up to a woman. Even when I was a kid it had been this way. The men would sit silently before the ballgame while the women chatted in the kitchen. The kitchen was where the conversation and food were.

I elaborated with Maridel: "It had to do with Dad, too. It was just easier to speak with Mom. Dad could go on too long and he could say strange or crude things. When I had something to discuss I saved it till Mom got home. But here's the funny thing. I haven't had a real conversation with Mom in years, not a really deep one."

"Why is that?"

"I didn't know. I remember once back in Battle Ground, a friend and I were standing in the lunch line. They were serving spaghetti. I said, 'I like it the way my mom makes it.'

"He said, 'You always say that.'

"I felt he'd found me out, that I was a mama's boy. I felt ashamed. After that I never said it again.

"There's something else, too, though. Maybe I haven't been able to open up to Mom because I resent her for putting Dad ahead of Tracey and me. Maybe she gave so much attention to him, that she ran short when it came to us. Maybe I didn't want her to leave Dad, but maybe part of me did—because life with him could be so hard."

31.

Stuc had a screening room for films. One night I went to see Bruce Weber's *Broken Noses*, about teenage boxers. I liked its unruly style, which was also visible on the poster. It showed Bruce and the boys giving us the finger. I took one of the posters and hung it on the outside of the door to my room. It didn't occur to me this might be inappropriate in a seminary. I figured the brothers would appreciate the joke. I was just trying to keep us real.

I also took some fake crap someone gave me in a box of chocolates—I wasn't the only one screwing around—and put it in one of the showers. You should have heard the commotion at breakfast. People swore it stunk. Some speculated it was revenge taken by a guy who'd been kicked out. Fun times!

These shenanigans escaped the notice of the powers-that-be, but I did get busted for one thing. During my assessment Tom brought up a point raised by the vice-rector. At the cocktail hour one Friday I'd tossed a paper airplane. Apparently two nuns had seen this. This reflected badly on the seminary and showed a lack of maturity on my part.

I frowned. "I'm not interested in tight-ass conformity."

Tom said, "Duly noted."

My restive spirit showed itself in a more abrasive form later that spring. It began innocently enough. A youth minister from a military base invited a priest, a fellow seminarian, and me to the base for a weekend visit. The priest would say Mass and the brother and I would speak to the youth group. After that we were invited to a barbecue. For our trouble we'd be paid a hundred bucks apiece. Sweet deal, we thought. But when we got there we found no arrangements had been made. We watched, embarrassed, as our host (a guy old enough to know better), asked families on the spot if they could put us up for the night. The youth group was surprised to see us, and by the time we got to the barbecue the food was gone. The youth minister was nowhere to be found and there was no payment.

On the drive home we were livid. I said I'd write the letter.

Later Tom said, "I read that letter. You cut his balls off."

Upon further reflection I realized there'd probably been a better way to handle it.

32.

The American College had a working relationship with US military bases in Belgium, Germany, and the Netherlands. Starting in our second year we were given pastoral assignments either on a base or at an international parish in Brussels or The Hague. (In our first year we took care of the community that came to mass at the seminary.) The military also offered pastoral assignments in the summer, and when spring came we began considering possible summer jobs. Since we were not supposed to return to the US in our first two years, working on a military base as a chaplain-candidate presented an enticing alternative. It paid well and gave you a chance to travel. If you signed up with the Navy you would sail to distant ports, and the Air Force offered placements on bases in Turkey and Greece. Wouldn't that be great, I thought, to serve as a second lieutenant, chaplain-candidate in Greece?

But Lordy, how many contradictions can a man hold within him? For if I balked at the restrictions of the seminary, why would I want to join the military? More to the point, what about all Dad's warnings of militarism and warfare? In high school I'd taken this to heart and registered as a conscientious objector. After my conversion I had come to greatly admire Dorothy Day's unwavering commitment to nonviolence. My own archbishop, Hunthausen, was a leading voice against the nuclear arms race. Hadn't Jesus himself renounced violence and said, "Turn the other cheek"? I'd absorbed all of these perspectives and made them truly my own.

But I knew there were more sides to the question, and more to me. The defense and protection of others is a legitimate moral end, and Jesus commended the centurion's faith without telling him to lay down arms. My grandfather had served in what I deemed to be a just cause (resisting fascism in World War II). Dad himself had had noble intentions (to resist communist domination) in what proved to be a more dubious cause in Vietnam.

I decided to apply for the Air Force program. It was about more than just earning money and living out some Chuck Yeager fantasy. When I asked for approval from the archdiocese, I explained it this way: Faith helped my father survive the war. Soldiers need people who remind them of Christ's presence and love.

33.

That business got me thinking a lot about Dad. He shared a dream with me once, about being sent out on a hopeless mission in Vietnam. He was on the road at night, always at night. There was a lot of dirt and wire. He was stranded in a village, surrounded by Viet

Cong, afraid he'd been left behind. The villagers stared at him with big eyes.

He'd had this dream repeatedly. He'd wake up drenched in sweat. Then his sweat would trigger Mom's.

One evening it hit home when the brothers and I watched a film. *Ordinary People*. It's the story of a family's struggle after the older son dies in a boating accident. The younger son Conrad is racked with guilt for not having been able to save him. I'd seen it in high school, but now I it seemed more pertinent than ever. I was fully engrossed in it when one of the brothers laughed. His laughter wasn't entirely out of place. In the scene we'd just watched Conrad's mother's had gone to absurd lengths to pretend everything was normal. But the laughter made me furious. I watched the movie to the end and then left without a word. I went to my room, buried my face, and wept bitter, bitter tears.

He wanted to die more than he wanted to live.

I remembered what Dad had said about his suicide attempt. When we were in Arizona he'd been hallucinating ghosts. Then he found himself, tail between his legs, back in Indiana. One night he started freaking out. He thought the devil was trying to capture Mom's and Grandma Mae's soul. Dad believed he had to enter the realm of the dead to fight for their souls.

Grandpa gave Dad some of his own medication to calm him down. Dad took off. He drove to Muncie to see Fr. Bates. Fr. Bates talked with him and tried to get him to stay, but he wouldn't.

Dad saw hitchhikers beside the road. "They were devils to me," he said. "I was turned on, just like in my track in Vietnam. I thought death was the answer. I thought people I loved had gone through it into a new life and left me behind."

At dawn he went to a hardware store and bought a chain. "There was no way out. I was on a termination mission. I took off my shoes. I walked as a repentant sinner. I saw a man tilling his field. I thought he would bury me."

Dad climbed a telephone pole. He wrapped one end of the chain around his neck and fastened the other to a foothold above. Then he launched himself.

See the man. He hangs between heaven and earth.

"When I woke I thought it was the resurrection. But I was alive in the same world.

"When I tried to get up, I couldn't. My back hurt and I realized I must still be dead. I thought I hadn't paid enough and my sufferings were just beginning."

The chain, designed to restrain a dog not hang a man, had broken. Dad crawled up to the road. A police car came. The officer checked him for needle tracks and called an ambulance.

34.

I cried that night in the seminary but didn't when Mom wrote in March saying Tracey was in the hospital. She'd overdosed on cocaine. Maybe by then I was done feeling. Maybe there was only so much feeling a man could do. Maybe I was just sick of it all, or thought this was the obvious outcome of bad choices she'd made (*Why do you always have to try everything? Why do you always have to dive in with the drowning?*), though I knew it was heartless to harbor such thoughts. What did I know about what she'd been through? After all, what did she know about me?

Life could be so disgusting. You wanted it to be so much that it wasn't. Why couldn't it all just work? God planted flowers and then buzzed them with his lawnmower.

But no, no, of course it was never *God's* fault, it was always your own. *My fault.* Dylan rebuking me: "O sister, am I not a brother to you?"

She had so much talent. Even after checking out of high school for a year she'd come back and immediately started kicking ass. In McLaughlin's English class, she'd scored a ten on her first essay. Word got back to me. I was proud of her but didn't say it. When I heard some girl was hassling her, I went to that girl and said, "Do me a favor. Lay off my sister." I was student body president then. I had a lot of clout. I did something, at least. Didn't I once in a while at least try to do something, Lord?

35.

Surprisingly—given my old nausea at the thought of him—I actually went to a Dylan concert that spring. He was playing in Brussels and a friend of mine had tickets. Over time I'd come to appreciate Dylan and thought this might be my last chance to see him. (This was before I realized rock stars never quit.) Speaking against this outing was the exam I was due to take the next morning, for which I was only minimally prepared. But what the hell. Going to a concert fit with my new devil-may-care, screw-it-all style.

The concert sucked, though. It was way too loud. I kept my fingers in my ears.

And eventually that exam period did stress me out. I drank milk at breakfast, but my stomach ached all morning. I dreaded the night before an exam. After dinner I'd get a burst of energy, but this faded quickly, while I still had lots to review. All I wanted to do was sleep. Psalm 104 summed it up: "You bring darkness on, night falls, all the forest animals come out."

But I got through it. Passed my exams, flew to Athens.

In my arrogance I assumed I'd done better than I actually had. Instead of a *cum laude* I had a *cum fructu*, "with fruit." Funny. Oh well, what the hell. Onward and upward!

36.

Being at the airbase in Athens took some getting used to. I felt like an impostor in my uniform, since I'd had no military training—no boot camp or anything close to that—and was now walking around being saluted by guys like the friendly chief master sergeant who had absolutely paid their dues. Often I didn't know whether I was supposed to salute or be saluted. But people were forgiving.

And it was fun. Fr. K., the chaplain, was hospitable. He took me out for ouzo and souvlaki and big mugs of beer. I got to preach, and families had me over for dinner. At the commissary I was able to stock up on American products. On the Fourth of July I drank Tang and read *As I Lay Dying*, writing Mom and Dad: "On Independence Day I find myself in the birthplace of democracy." Best of all was meeting Ed, an Army captain and doctor who'd graduated from West Point and was now working in the E.R. Ed was Catholic and very amusing. He made sure I never got bored. When his roommate moved out, he let me have the room rent-free. When Sung arrived I was feeling great.

37.

Flush with traveler's checks and our Eurail passes, Sung and I left Athens on the 24th of August. Does wearing a backpack make you an explorer? Was civilization now a wilderness? It sure felt like it.

The glory of it was deciding on a whim where to go. One night we slept in a town without even knowing its name. The next we slept on the deck of the boat that brought us from Patras to Brindisi. In Italy our train came to a stop in a sea of vegetation. The leaves came right in the windows.

I loved little stations with no one else there. Just sitting and waiting in the heat, surrounded by grass and crickets.

Our plan, to the extent there was one, was to proceed from Athens to Leuven by way of Italy, France, Germany and wherever else we decided to go.

38.

In the end much of what we did was what all the backpackers did. We read our guidebook, stayed in hostels, admired famous places, took pictures, and tried to look cool. That we were not unique was shown by our repeated encounters with some girls from Mexico. "Hola!" We met them in the train from Brindisi to Rome, then by chance a day later at St. Peter's, a week later in Florence, and three weeks later in Amsterdam.

Being with Sung was a blast. Just being a regular guy again, out there and seeing stuff. He brought me a Pike Place Market t-shirt and two books: a collection of Raymond Carver stories (this wonderful writer was buried in our own Port Angeles) and *The Unbearable Lightness of Being*. At Shakespeare and Company in Paris I picked up Sam Shepard's *Motel Chronicles*. I chronicled our adventures in my journal. What a time!

Sung was doing well, getting on with his life. His roommate said to me once, "He's like a freight train." He was preparing for law school and paving the way for his future career as a political strategist. The people he was friends with now would later be elected officials in Seattle and Olympia. Besides seeing stuff, Sung was interested in eating good food on our trip. He didn't need a girlfriend, he already had one.

39.

Sung had places he definitely wanted to see, but it didn't matter much to me. I thought we might spend a night at a monastery, which would be cheap, but then I thought better of it. We'd be expected to join in the prayer. The one place I was sure I wanted to visit was in the French Pyrenees, a spot called Thuès-Entre-Valls. Noëmi's family owned a rustic inn there for travelers. She said she would be there herself at some point. So after Rome and Florence and a stay at a dumpy place in La Spezia, we hugged the Mediterranean, alternating delightful views with stretches of tunnel. We pulled into Perpignan at 5:30 on a Saturday morning.

Though we had no francs, we decided to press on, since the exchange wouldn't be open until 9:00. We figured we could change money at Olette, near the inn, but when we got there no one wanted our dollars. I tried calling Noëmi's brother, Thomas—she'd said he'd be there—but no one picked up. Rather than wait for the next train, we decided to hoof it. It was only six kilometers. If we couldn't change money at the house, it was still early enough to get a train back to where we could.

The road to Thuès-Entre-Valls reminded me of the Hurricane Ridge Road: high, winding, and exposed. It was beautiful but hot. We had our packs but no water. The tunnels gave relief from the sun, but we worried the cars wouldn't see us in time.

After two hours we arrived at our destination. It was not as we imagined. We weren't even sure we were in the right place. There was no sign and the caretaker spoke no English. When I said, "Noëmi," he looked at me blankly. "Thomas" rang a bell though.

"Later," he said. He led us to the barn and pointed to some bunk beds. We dropped our packs and took a nap.

When I woke, I realized we'd missed the train to nearby Prades, or Perpignan if necessary, to change money. We had no food, and without money you can't buy it.

A dark cloud formed in my head.

And then, as quickly as it came, the cloud disappeared. For as I wandered the property I met a lovely French girl, Cathy. But that's not how she said it. She said Cathy the French way, which is a way that makes you want to sleep with her every day for the rest of your life.

Right here, in the middle of nowhere. When I'm starving. Who cares about food?

She gave me an inquisitive look. We were alone on a desert island.

But no, we were not. She and her parents were just leaving. I could ride along, though, to Prades. "The banks will be closed, but you can change money at the station."

I left a note for Sung, who was still sleeping.

During the drive, I sought to learn more. Would she be coming back? Alas.

They let me out. "Good luck!"

As luck would have it, the exchange was closed. "The desk in Perpignan is still open," the stationmaster said, "but by the time you get there it will be closed."

I sat on a bench by the tracks. This was just the kind of place I loved—empty and lost. Loved when I had a belly full of food, that is. We still hadn't eaten anything and now I was headed back without food or francs. And tomorrow was Sunday.

I sat in silence wondering, *What now?*

If the hunger and futility had been all, the moment would not have been significant. Sung and I were not going to starve in the Pyrenees. At most this would be an anecdote for later. But sometimes you look back at a moment of your life and realize there was more to it. Something changed. Now when I see myself alone under that blue sky in France I know my story took a decisive turn. Every time I think of it I hear the opening bars of Copland's "Appalachian Spring"—so soft and mournful and hopeful at the same time.

I heard a man's voice. He was speaking English to a woman who'd just stepped off a train.

"Are you American?" I asked.

"I am," he said.

He didn't have many francs on him, but gave me twenty for three dollars.

I bought bread, meat, and oranges, and caught the next train up the mountain.

As we pulled away, I remembered why I knew the name Prades. It was the birthplace of Thomas Merton.

40.

In my first week in the seminary, I'd wondered where the women were. Soon enough though I'd found them in Leuven, and now I saw they were in in every nook, cranny, aisle, and stairwell of Europe. Hearing me go on about Cathy, Sung said, "You're a live rooster!" After that he started giving me shit every time I even looked at a girl. "Three more weeks of celibacy for me," he said, "but fifty more years for you."

Girls like Sandrine, another *française*, loitering, as I was, in the walkway of the train. It was so easy to talk to her, and so painful to watch her walk away. And Anke, a German who was studying in Cologne. We met her in Heidelberg. She had it all, I thought. She was beautiful, smart, and training to be a doctor. Cologne wasn't far from Leuven. We would have to keep in touch. *Wait, what am I talking about? I'm a seminarian, dammit!*

By the time we got to Leuven, I was tired of being on the road. Noëmi met us for lunch at the Old Market. She apologized for having missed us in France. She laughed when she heard our story. She said she was looking forward to the start of classes. As she left we watched in admiration as she swung her hip over the saddle of her bike. She was what Johnny Cash would have called a "swingin' maid." Sung looked around at all the terraces full of girls. He shook his head. "Putting a seminary here is like putting a fox in with the chickens."

41.

My new room at the seminary was a step up from my spartan domicile of the year before. It had a better bed and view. My new neighbor was Bob L., one of the most straight-laced guys in the seminary—in any seminary! He frowned when he saw the Air Force hadn't shaped me up. Indeed, I was more rickety than ever. I liked Bob, though, for while I knew I put his patience to the test—with hockey games on the hall, for example (we used a duct-taped roll of toilet paper for a puck)—I discerned amusement beneath his chastisement. Reading my situation correctly, Bob told Al, who was closer to me, that he should try to help. But Al, who I'd already told of my struggle, had said he couldn't help me. It hit too close to home.

After a while, I settled down. Routine helped. Morning prayer, mass. I remembered the many reasons I wanted to be a priest, and thought of all the people back home who were rooting for me. Like Ray and Jan, friends of Fr. Michael's, who'd sent me a hundred dollars to help meet expenses. And kids from camp. And Grandma, who was always praying for me and having mass offered for me.

Fr. Michael had said: Falling in love is just part of the package for a priest. He'd experienced it more than once. "It happens in marriage, too," he said. "All of us have to choose again and again to be faithful."

I have come this far. Maybe my summer of freedom has aired me out.

It was time to refocus.

42.

Over at Stuc I ran into the Red One. "The meals at Poverello are too good for the poor," he said. "I've got friends who eat from garbage cans." I couldn't quite follow his logic. Alongside him was

Robert, another regular from the soup kitchen. He'd had a lot to drink. Between that and my limited Dutch I only understood half of what he said.

Stuc was always full of Bohemian-types. Many studied politics and sociology. They all dressed in black, except for their jeans, and rolled their own cigarettes. It was always smoky in there. As in all the Belgian cafés, Stuc served alcohol as well as coffee, and kids and dogs were welcome. It was everything all together, with big windows on two sides and Billy Bragg blasting, "You're an accident waiting to happen."

Every so often someone took a chair from my table. When people left for class the guy at the counter would return the chairs. I just kept writing away.

43.

One afternoon the rector stopped by as I was cleaning up my room. "I have an idea, the perfect thing for someone who likes to write. For your house job this year I'd like you to edit our newsletter."

"I'm flattered," I said, "but I really like the job I have now." Mike and I were the grounds crew. We cut the grass and raked the leaves. It was good to be outside, whereas Tom's proposal sounded like an office job, one step closer to the chancery. Archbishop Murphy, Seattle's coadjutor who was now in charge of seminarians, had already urged Dennis to coax me back into the STB program.

But I gave in to Tom's request. It wasn't important enough to make a stink about. And it proved to be a fun assignment. My first piece profiled the new arrivals. These were men, I said (quoting *Hebrews*), "who by faith conquered kingdoms, did what was just, and obtained the promises; they broke the jaws of lions, put out raging fires, and escaped the devouring sword." Laying it on and loving it!

Some of the new guys I could relate to—like Paul D., who'd studied literature and wrote poetry, and Geno, who'd knocked himself out keeping up his grades while rowing crew for Holy Cross. But one guy mystified me with his responses. It was as though every answer was calculated not to say anything. When we were done he said, "You'll let me see what you write, of course." I assured him I would. I thanked him and said to let me know if I could ever be of help.

He said, "I'm sure you will more than you will ever know."

Afterwards I laughed. It gave me the creeps!

44.

From the beginning, what has sustained me most in my faith has been the eucharist. I suppose that was the main thing that drew me to the seminary, though I wasn't especially aware of it. Soon after I first started attending mass a Catholic friend at Princeton had said, "Are the sacraments important to you?"

I guess he'd noticed I didn't receive communion. I was too embarrassed to say I didn't know what a sacrament was. (This was before I had received instruction, and Princeton students don't like to admit they don't know something.) I just said, "Well, I think it's beautiful."

What was beautiful was the simplicity of word and gesture and the outrageous thought of God dying and giving himself to us as food.

Over time I saw that the liturgy was like a play or good story. It involved you, drew you in, implicated you morally—as happened when the prophet Nathan told his story to sinful David. What changed in the mass finally wasn't just the bread and wine, but, ideally, your own heart, which turned from stone to flesh.

God, not the priest, was the true presider. By means of the mass he led you deeper into the mystery of love.

Maybe it was a sign that I rarely imagined myself saying mass. I didn't need to lead it, I just needed to be close to it.

45.

One Friday Noëmi and I walked in the woods before she left town for the weekend. The forest, south of town, was called *Zoet Water* (Sweet Water). I'd known the place since my first week in Leuven, when I'd explored it with a guidebook. I'd learned then that dandelions, in Dutch, are called *paardebloemen*, horse flowers. I thought that was funny, just as it was funny that Dutch roosters say *kuku-luku*, instead of cock-a-doodle-doo, like they do in America.

The colors were muted. Though late in October, it was still warm. We found a dry spot in a clearing where we could sit. It was nice to talk without being interrupted and on display. Back in town I always felt someone was looking over my shoulder when I spoke to a girl. We leaned back and studied the sky. I asked about her family. She had auburn hair and a long white neck. I told her I'd been struggling, but now felt I was back on track.

As we walked back to the bus stop, she said, "You know, you can't do this as a priest."

It surprised and annoyed me.

"What?"

"This." I knew she was right. Though I was telling myself we were only talking—*Wasn't this a perfect example of non-sexual intimacy?*—I knew it was more than that, and I wanted it to be more. To make a habit of this as a priest would be hurt the woman, hurt myself, and hurt those I would serve.

We boarded the bus.

46.

If seminaries stand one step removed from "the world," monasteries are even more so, and this was particularly true of Clervaux in Luxembourg, where my growth group retreated right after Thanksgiving. The train followed the river and let us out at the foot of the hill atop which the monastery lay shrouded in mist. The brothers and I climbed through woods where soldiers had faced off in the Battle of the Bulge. A portly guest master welcomed us, pulling chocolates and liqueurs from a cabinet and, seemingly, his robe. After serving coffee he showed us our rooms. At three we joined the monks in the chapel. There we found Tom Ivory, who'd traveled separately. We'd asked him to lead the retreat.

Dom Jean Leclercq, OSB sat down with us after our first conference. I knew his book *The Love of Learning and Desire for God*. Leclercq was old and lively. He told us he'd known Thomas Merton, and had been with him at the conference in Thailand where

Merton had died. "I'm very enthusiastic about humankind," he said. "I hear there are bad people, but I never meet them." When he said that I decided it was because he lived in an abbey, but the more I've thought about it since, it seems to apply to my own life as well. Have I ever known anyone truly bad? I mean, we're all screwy, and some seriously so, but still . . .

Before sleeping that night I read Psalm 43: "Why so downcast, my soul? Why do you sigh within me?" The room was cold. I was glad for the extra wool blanket. I pulled it up around my ears.

What did I want from this retreat? Usually on retreats I had something I wanted to pray about or something I wanted to read, but now I felt blank, empty. I thought about how far east I was. Dad had taken us west, even west of what most Americans thought of as "the West," and here I was now, east of East. Why? To reverse the process? To flee? To fix it all?

Why are monasteries so stony? Does prayer need stone?

47.

In the morning I walked at the first opportunity, after Prime but before the first conference. The bare-limbed trees reminded me of two photographs: a shot of Merton in the woods in *The Sign of Jonas* and Edouard Boubat's photo of children in the snow at Luxembourg Gardens in Paris.

I said little during the conferences. Afterwards I read: "My soul still seeks, and has not found" (*Ecclesiastes* 7:28). And

> Three things are too wonderful for me,
>   yes, four I cannot understand:
> The way of an eagle in the air,
>   the way of a serpent upon a rock,
> The way of a ship on the high seas,
>   and the way of a man with a maiden.
>   —*Proverbs* 30:18–19

Tom found me after Mass, alone in the chapel, crying.
I told him I just couldn't do it.

48.

Ordinarily, I would not have gone home that Christmas. My first trip would have been in the summer. But the rector agreed it made sense for me to see my family and talk things over with Archbishop Murphy. Dad bought me the ticket. His first disability payment had arrived.

We celebrated the Feast of the Immaculate Conception, the feast day of the College, shortly before I left. We did this, as usual, with mass, followed by drinks and a banquet. I decided I was going to live it up this time, really have some fun. The new *Esquire* contained a slew of Christmas jokes, which I shared in the course of the evening. ("How is a priest like a Christmas tree? They both wear their balls for decoration.") The priests and seminarians at table were already well-oiled. It didn't take much to get them going. But the elderly Belgian woman who sat at our table—she was an old friend of the seminary, like my grandmother she washed the liturgical vestments—squirmed as the boys roared at my pilfered jokes. "My ears are burning," she said.

Later, after the *pousse café*—that is, after the drink after the coffee that followed all the other drinks—some of us gathered up in Mike's room to keep the fun going. Seeing Mike's basket of laundry (clean, luckily), I grabbed a pair of his boxer shorts and put them on my head. "Look, I'm the king," I said.

Seeing my state of disintegration, Spaldo—who is now a bishop, and a fine bishop I'm sure he is—took pity. He said, "Come on, Timbo. I'll walk you home." Which he did, leading me down the stairs to my room, asking before leaving, "Are you doing okay?"

"You know," I said, "you're about the only guy who's asked. There've been times I've wept in pain in that chapel and no one came to me. No one said a word."

He said, "We don't always see what's going on, or know what a guy needs."

Good point. How many guys had I reached out to and tried to understand in my time in the seminary?

49.

When I got home, Mom said, "It sounds like the same old thing."

"What's that?" I said.

"Your struggle with celibacy."

And yes, that was certainly the main thing. It took so much energy to do celibacy properly that I was burning out before I even started in ministry. I wasn't one to cut corners, or fake it. If I was going to be a priest, I wanted to do it by the book, which meant not only no sexual relations but also no masturbation, if I could help it. Sometimes I felt like a shook-up Coke bottle. I tried sublimating in prayer, but I don't know . . . Maybe it works for some people.

I missed romance, intimacy, touch. Beyond that longing, however, I'd also discovered something else that would make priesthood for me difficult, given my personality. A parish priest is a very public figure, always on call. I'd come to realize just how much an introvert I am. Could someone like me connect with people all day? It sounded exhausting. Oh man, how could I have ever imagined myself a politician?

50.

While in Port Angeles, I dropped in on the Turners. Suzanne was home from her senior year at Stanford. Two guys in her class— friends from college, both pursuing her—had just been there for a visit. Who would win her hand? I thought it was a funny situation.

Mrs. Turner made some hot chocolate with whipped cream. Suzanne and I sat down to watch "Miracle on 34th Street." When we got to the part where St. Nicholas speaks to the little girl in Dutch, I translated. Suzanne said, "If you hadn't gone over there, you wouldn't be able to do that."

I felt at ease with her now. It had been a painful before, when I'd dreamed of a future with her and that didn't work out. When I let that hope go, I told her it was the biggest dream I'd ever had. But once I'd done so, I'd been at peace with it and had accepted it. Now we were just friends. So much so, in fact, that I stretched out on the couch and put my legs across her lap. Just like that, in proprietary fashion. I laughed inside, thinking how jealous her beaus would be if they knew. Suzanne didn't say anything. She just watched the movie.

On the 27th of December, Dr. Turner, Suzanne, Shelley, and I left before dawn to hike up to Lake Angeles. We arrived to find the air white and the lake a sea of green glass. We were surrounded by mountains. The ice was perfectly smooth. Dr. Turner brought along hockey sticks and a puck.

A fall left me with a nice bruise on my hip. It had been a while since I'd skated, but on that day I came as close as I ever would to being graceful on ice.

When we got back to the house, Mrs. Turner served us pancakes with raspberries.

51.

Archbishop Murphy listened sympathetically. He said he was sorry I wouldn't be continuing, and agreed with my proposal to finish out the year at the seminary. Since I'd switched to the BA-MA track, I would be awarded a BA in Religious Studies at the end of this year. At least I would have a diploma to show for my time in Leuven. Maybe, I thought, I could get a job with Catholic Charities, or write for the diocesan paper.

52.

In Leuven I found myself more at ease, and I saw the people around me anew. Instead of being annoyed with brothers focused on vestments and the Burgundian good life, I laughed at these things. No, I still didn't think that was what priesthood should be about, but having seen the absurdity of my own quest (Was there ever a more unlikely seminarian?), I decided life was as Bruegel painted it: a carnival of folly.

Two things did, however, make my final months in the seminary a challenge. The first was the need to pass exams. Theoretically, this shouldn't have been a big deal. My courses weren't particularly difficult. All I had to do was put in the time. Unfortunately, though, a misstep in January put me on edge for the rest of the year. I failed my canon law exam. This resulted not from a lack of study, but from studying in the wrong way. Since the professor had said it would be an open-book exam, I'd marked up my codex accordingly and thought I was good to go. But when I got in there, I saw it was an oral exam like any other. I could consult the book on some specific point, but essentially I needed to have everything memorized like always. When he asked the first question, I just looked at him.

He said, "Did you study for this exam?"

Not good. Having failed it, I could still pass the year, but failing a second one, in June, would be fatal.

The other troubling thing was impatience. I was almost out of the seminary, but not quite. And as Sung had noted, there were a lot of good-looking women in Leuven.

Now if it is difficult being a seminarian under these circumstances, it is also difficult, surely, being the rector supervising such a seminarian. And all the more difficult when you have befriended said seminarian, which was the case now between Tom and me. Since I had opened up to him, in my first weeks in the seminary, he had also opened up to me, sharing some of his own struggles. Our visit to Naples together had built upon that. I think Tom saw something of himself in me, and I think he was lonely.

53.

A letter from Mom brought hopeful news of Tracey, who was trying to make a new start. Along with that Mom enclosed an update on the crisis surrounding Fr. Bruce Ritter. He'd been accused by a young man of sexual misconduct. When the father of the accuser called his son a chronic liar, I'd hoped the accusation might not be true. But now a second accuser had come forward. Fr. Ritter had stepped down.

On my way to Stuc I ran into a woman I knew from Poverello. She used to come there with her husband and baby, but now, she told me, she and her child were in a shelter. Her husband was looking for her, and I was not to say I'd seen her.

I wondered if I'd ever seen her smile.

54.

With this chapter of my life drawing to a close, I considered what I'd learned during my five years of discernment. Thanks to Channel and my conversations with psychologists, I knew I had a better grasp of how my family history had shaped me. I'd tried hard to compensate for Dad's lack of success. I saw, too, that I had asked too much of women. I'd worshiped them and looked to them to save me. That's not a good basis for a relationship. Trusting in God and embracing celibacy, difficult as it had been, had put me on more stable footing. Most importantly, I'd realized there are needs inside one that only God can meet.

Had I become any holier? Probably not, since I equated holiness with selflessness, but maybe a little if holiness has to do with spiritual health. I was more balanced than I had been. Maybe now I had a better foundation for loving people in the future.

So there went my youth. I was not a senator or a saint. What was I instead? Just a guy, I guess.

Looking down from a bridge into the Dijle, I laughed. It occurred to me that I could follow this little river out to the North Sea, across the Atlantic, and up the Mississippi, Ohio, and Wabash back to the bank where I used to dream at riverside. I'd always thought the Wabash was an Indiana river, not something connected to everything else.

55.

In April Tom asked if I wanted to join him on a trip to Norway. One of the brothers, Keith, accompanied us as far as Copenhagen. When we parted, Keith laughed, "Have fun."

"What did he mean by that?" Tom asked.

"I don't know," I said, though Keith seemed to be expressing my own doubts about the trip. I wasn't sure it was a good idea, but how could I pass on a chance to see Scandinavia when Tom was paying for gas and lodging? Still, four days was a long time to socialize. I liked Tom, and we generally could find stuff to talk about, but I was eager to be on my own. If I met a pretty Swede, I sure didn't want the rector in tow.

In Gothenberg, I suggested we split up for a few hours. I wanted to write in a café. He said, "What the hell? I thought we were traveling together."

We made it through that trip unscathed—keeping on the move helped—but in the months that followed I chafed increasingly at the restrictions of the seminary. I bristled whenever Tom said, "How's it going?"

The worst were days with formation classes in the evening on top of all the rest we had to do. At every opportunity, I stole away to Stuc. There one girl in particular intrigued me, a blond who for some reason had recently died her hair black. Then after a while she was back to being blond again.

Who was she like? I tried to place her. Well, Brigitte Bardot for one. Sexy and cool, and very European, with almond shaped eyes. Her way of carrying herself brought to mind those faucets we used to have out on the river. They ran hot and cold at the same time. You felt the water mixing.

She was always with some other girl. That girl looked pretty good, too.

56.

All I had left were the exams. Nine of them crammed into sixteen days. Just the studying. Highlighting the notes. Making the outline based on the highlights. Reducing it all to five key words. Unpacking those five words when the time came. That's all I had to do, nine times over.

I buckled down, studying in my room, studying at the library, studying at Stuc.

When that girl—I heard someone call her Janke—came in with her friend, I said, The next time she comes in alone, I'm going to talk to her.

57.

Christology. Check! Letters of Paul. Check! Sacraments. Check! Three exams down, six to go.

In Philosophy of Religion, I rubbed my hands together when I saw the question: "What are three things a God-believer can learn from an atheist?"

Hell, I could riff on that one all day. So much of what I knew from my days of unbelief benefitted my faith now. My earlier atheism had, for one thing, made me wary of easy answers and theological jargon. It had shown me the fine line between faith and craziness, and how death is ever on the prowl, seeking to devour us while leaving us seemingly alive. I don't know any more what all I said to the professor, but he just looked at me after my answer and said, "Those are not the three things."

When Spaldo saw me, he said, "How did it go?"

I said, "Mark, when you play the game the way I do, you learn to accept a level of risk."

He said, "You know you're supposed to put only one bullet in the gun, right, not six?"

58.

You never know when the day will come. It just comes. Suddenly you're in the day. I went to Stuc, just like every other Wednesday, and there she was, for the first time alone.

Now where is that other girl?

The white-hot focus of my desire was present and available. She wore a peachy shirt. She of the clear-as-a-bell face and all-the-stars-of-the-sky blue eyes. I looked down at my coffee. If I left it here it would get cold. *Are you a man or are you a mouse?*

"Do you mind if I join you?"

She was reading the paper. She glanced up, made a little room, and proceeded to ignore me.

I introduced myself. I said, "I've been here for two years. I've probably seen you a hundred times. I'll be leaving soon, but I've always wanted to talk to you. I thought if I didn't do it now I'd always regret it."

She said, "You come here a lot?"

I nodded.

"That's funny, I've never seen you before."

She didn't know seminarians even still existed.

Before she left she asked, "Will you be at the *Einddagen*?" That's was Stuc's year-end blowout.

I said, "Will you?"

59.

I was at Stuc early and was sure it was not going to work out. How could it? This sort of thing never worked out.

I got a pint of Stella and stood outside listening to the band, shivering. I thought, "I can't be shivering when she shows up. *If* she shows up." Then Miche from Poverello showed up. Sometimes we worked together. I was glad to have someone to talk to, so I wouldn't look like I didn't have any friends. I asked what had led her to volunteer, looking around as I listened. Then to my surprise, I saw her. Or rather *it*, my lifeline: a swinging rope of gold—her braided hair, brushing the back of her skirt.

I said, "Excuse me, Miche, I've got to do something."

Janke said, "Oh there you are."

She *had* come. I couldn't believe it.

Later, Miche came over to me, quite drunk, with a sad look on her face. "Tim, I need to speak with you."

I had a pretty good idea what this was about. Someone's else's dream was not working out at the very moment that mine was, and maybe for the same reason.

I said, "Miche, I'm sorry, but I can't do this right now."

She looked at me pleadingly. "Please, Tim."

"I'm sorry."

After the party, Janke and her friend Nancy and I got French onion soup in a café. They were both Dutch, not Flemish.

60.

A day later Janke was, as she said she'd be, studying at the main library. I approached her with my books.

She said, "Go away, because I have to study. But you can come to dinner." She gave me her address.

Her room was a mess—we couldn't find the corkscrew—but she was a great cook. I studied her ass as she stood at the stove. We had quiche, and strawberries for desert.

Outside, on the stoop, I said, "Will you slap me if I kiss you?"

She said, "No, but I wouldn't advise it."

Then, as we walked back up the steps, she said, "I can't believe I'm doing this."

She had a compact, ripe-to-bursting sexiness about her, a light-footed, feline grace. If a nearly-ex seminarian had to date a girl from a Guess ad, she would be the one you would want. (Why were American girls so reluctant to show cleavage?)

61.

Tom saw me with a big grin on my face. "What are you so happy about?"

"I've met an amazing woman."

She loved to study in the sun. I studied with her whenever I could.

Janke didn't always know when I was joking and when I was being serious. When Paul met her, he loved how she deflated my big ideas with her sharp remarks.

With Janke there was never any guessing. You always knew exactly where you stood. During a tour of our chapel, she told me there were too many colors in the windows. Seeing me once in a pair of wool trousers, she said, "You should put those in the closet and get them out when you're eighty years old."

She put me at ease. There was no need for strategizing. She said what she thought and did what she said. No games, what a relief! Not a one, from the very beginning, and to this day.

62.

A week later, on Saturday, Tom and I played racquetball. Racquet-ball was good for getting out your frustrations: slamming the ball, crashing into the wall, doing your damnedest to beat your oppo-nent. We had a weight room at the seminary, which was good, but I regretted it had no punching bag.

After the game Tom and I drank a soda, as we always did, before walking back to the College. I didn't have much to say. What was there to say? How awesome Janke was? How I couldn't wait to see her again?

Tom said, "So how was the party last night?"

Something in his tone put me on edge. It was the sarcastic way he said "party." That and the fact that I had no idea what he was referring to.

I said, "What party?"

He said, "Whose bed did you sleep in?"

My first thought was, *He checked my room. I wasn't at morn-ing prayer, so he checked my room.*

I was furious. Lots of guys skipped morning prayer on Sat-urday, and not just guys who were on their way out, but guys who were sure to be ordained. Normally I was one of the more faithful ones in my attendance.

"You weren't at prayer," he said, "so I knocked on your door. I thought you might be sick."

That he was concerned about my health was, I knew, utter bullshit. I knew he wasn't looking in other guys' rooms when they didn't show up. And he wouldn't have even known about Janke at all if I hadn't shared it within our friendship. I let him have it. "You are not my father," I said. "I already have a father. I don't need you, and I don't need the f-ing Catholic Church!"

But I didn't say the "effing" Catholic Church, I said the actual f-word, the one word Grandma told me she hated, and I used it against the Church she loved, the Church that *I* loved, the Church that had sustained me.

We finished the walk in silence.

63.

I wasn't exactly thrilled at the idea of trying to make a long-distance relationship work with Janke. I'd been through that before, and Seattle-to-Leuven is a very long distance indeed. She was only in her first year at the university, and so would be there for at least another three years. But she promised to write, and said she might visit at Christmas. I said I hoped she would.

And so I said goodbye to the American College. I did so with no wistfulness. It was the right thing. It was time.

Or *almost* said goodbye, for as fate would have it, the American College reunion was, coincidentally, being held in Seattle that year, and Fr. John Pinette, a friend and fellow alum (I was now officially an alumnus), was in charge. He'd asked if I could help out, earning a few bucks for myself in the process. I'd agreed. But that wasn't all. Earlier in the year, when the location of the reunion had been announced, Tom had said he would be attending. "Maybe I can come to Port Angeles and meet your parents." That had seemed fine when he'd mentioned it. But now the last thing I wanted was to spend more time with the rector just as I was getting out of the seminary. He and I had patched things up, without apologizing in so many words (he'd even met Janke, and was friendly), but the tension between us remained.

64.

From here on out I would be paying my own way. No longer did I have parents or an institution (Princeton, Channel, the Archdiocese) providing room and board. I would need a job, and quick. I scheduled a meeting with the director of Seattle's Catholic Community Services. Hearing that, Tom offered to loan me money, to buy a suit.

"That's generous of you," I said. We went to Nordstrom, where he was impressed by the service.

It took me years to pay him back. And not for lack of money either. Sometimes forgiveness takes time.

65.

After the reunion in Seattle, Tom and I walked onto the Bainbridge ferry. Mom and Dad met us on the other side. Not quite trusting their own car, they'd borrowed a friend's, which besides being dependable was bigger. Bainbridge to Port Angeles is a 90-minute drive. Tom and I sat in the back. We spoke of the reunion, of Seattle, of Leuven, of Tom's background, and my plans. Then Dad started telling us about spaceships and pyramids, and a vision he'd had of a phoenix rising. As he waded through his thoughts, I got increasingly agitated. Even for me this was new. Dad had many times over the years shared ideas that were farfetched, but normally he'd stayed within the bounds of the more-or-less recognizable, natural world, and when he spoke of what is beyond he couched it in conventionally religious terms. Now he seemed to be spinning loose in the cosmos, and I was desperate to reel him in. It wasn't just embarrassment on my part. I was genuinely concerned about his mental health. I thought I'd better get him back in touch with reality. So I started challenging him, pressing him, saying, "I don't know about that, Dad," and "Where's the evidence?" my remarks bristling with warning.

Tom, however, approached it differently. He said, "So you had this experience. What does it mean to you?" He was approaching it patiently, "pastorally," in the best sense of that word.

I shut up and stared out the window.

66.

Tom stayed with us two nights before returning to Seattle to sail to Alaska. He'd signed on as chaplain of a cruise ship. Being with him and Mom and Dad pushed my patience to the limit. I didn't want to be with Tom, and was afraid of what Dad might say.

We drove up to Hurricane Ridge and then out to the Elwha for a cookout. I tried to focus on the river, to let my mind just go with it. It was good to smell the Douglas Fir again.

Perhaps all would have run its course peacefully were it not for a stop we made on the way home. Dad wanted to say hello to a couple they'd gotten to know, Earl and Char, the people who'd loaned them the car. Earl, like Dad, was a Vietnam vet; Char was his wife; and they were both parishioners at Queen of Angels. I did not see the point of this stop, could not imagine how it could possibly be interesting for Tom, and certainly wanted no part of it myself. On the contrary: I was about to pop from my need to be on my own. But Dad ignored my protest. He pulled over, knocked on the door, and we all tromped inside.

Earl and Char welcomed us graciously. "Sit down! Would you like some coffee?" Everyone took a seat but me. I stood by the door, arms folded, and waited.

67.

On his last day, Tom and I went down to the waterfront. We sat on driftwood and talked. Then he went to make a phone call. When he came back, he said, "How badly do you want that degree?"

He'd spoken with the seminary. I'd failed three exams. I could retake them in August, and was even allowed to do this at a distance, but it meant I would have to study. Otherwise no BA from Leuven.

I put Tom on the bus. He said he'd be in touch.

When I got back to Mom and Dad's, I sat on the curb by the alley. Hearing me arrive, Dad came out and joined me. He was livid.

"I have *never* been rude to your friends," he said. "Ever."

He was right. Though I'd often been embarrassed by his appearance or something he'd said, he had always bent over backwards not to shame me in front of my friends. And now after all these years of isolation, when he himself was finally coming out and making some new friends—him and Mom both—I'd been totally rude to them.

We sat in silence. Then he flicked his hand and I flinched.

"What?!" he said.

I said, "I thought you were going to hit me."

He said, "Are you kidding? I was batting a fly. Have I *ever* hit you?"

It was my hesitation that did it. Hesitation because, while no, he'd never hit me in the sense he meant, he *had* spanked me any number of times, and I flashed back to a time he'd thrown a glass at me when I'd lipped off. More pertinent, though, were the countless times I'd walked on eggshells because of the *threat* of violence he presented. With Dad you never knew for sure that he could remain calm and peaceful. Taking my hesitation for a "Yes," he grabbed me by the collar, lifted me up, and drove me down onto the pavement. He climbed atop me and balled his fist at my face.

I stayed calm, the way I almost always was with him. There we were, looking at each other. I said, "Dad, what are you doing?"

It was as though I were outside myself, watching us from above.

A woman passing by stopped to look. Dad turned to her. "Haven't you ever seen a veteran with PTSD before?"

"It's all right," I said. Dad got off and went back inside.

I stood up and brushed myself off. *That's it. I'm done. I'm outta here. It's over.*

The End of the Road

I didn't leave that day. I didn't grab my stuff and catch the next bus to Seattle and turn my back on the old life—on everything that had ever frustrated me about my family and myself. What would be the point? It would all still be with me.

Instead I stayed a couple more days as planned, and then went over to Seattle to look for a job. Sung and I got an apartment together. When nothing turned up at Catholic Community Services or the diocesan paper, Sung's girlfriend got me on at Charlie's on Broadway, as a waiter. I retook the three exams and got my degree. At Espresso Roma, the closest thing to Stuc in the U District, I wrote Janke four letters a week. To my amazement, she wrote back, two to my every four. And then at Christmas she (again) really did come. I took her over to meet Mom and Dad. Dad said a few things you wouldn't expect somebody's dad to say to you, but Janke rolled with it, as she always would, with me and my family and our ways.

Probably if I had been the same age as Janke when I met her it would not have worked out. I needed the few years I had on her to become as balanced as she already was. When I left the formation program, Fr. Meyer warned, "Don't marry the first girl you meet." That's probably, in general, good advice. But in my case I didn't follow it and it worked out beautifully. I spent two years at Charlie's, saved my money and then went back to Leuven to complete the MA in theology, not as a seminarian now, but as just one more student in town. In 1994 Janke and I finished up there (she with a degree in physical therapy), and a week after graduating we got married in her hometown, Heemstede, the Netherlands. Then we moved to Washington State, where we lived for seven years. After our daughter Annegien was born Janke got the itch to return to her native land, so in 2001 we moved to Utrecht. I had already begun work on a doctoral dissertation. In 2003 I defended in practical theology at the Catholic Theological University of Utrecht. Our son Pieter was born a month later. Janke completed a PhD in physical therapy in 2010. We've been married thirty years. We still live in Utrecht. She works as a researcher and consultant and I serve on the staff of national pastoral resource center for parishes.

Being with Janke has grounded me. She is smart, loving, and a straight shooter. One thing she said early on was, "Why do you always quote other people when you write? Why don't you just say what *you* have to say?" It got me thinking about how I'd emulated so many people, from Daniel Boone on through FDR, Thomas Merton, and Dorothy Day. It began to sink in that maybe my calling wasn't to be a blurry copy of someone else, but finally, truly myself. Telling this story has been part of that process.

Sometimes I get down on myself because I'm not a bigtime crusader for peace and justice. I feel I'm letting people down. But when I ask myself what "doing it right," according to my own expectations, would look like, I realize I would only be satisfied by providing a global, structural solution to poverty and injustice that included compassionate, personal attention to individual needs. Only if I could do all that (while remaining humble in the process!) would I feel I'd done it right. No wonder Fr. Weiser underscored my use of the word "perfect"; Dr. Reilly said, "Don't give yourself so many missions"; and Maridel said, "There you go, like a little god!"

So I try to forgive myself, and settle for doing what I can—like the time I helped my parents and sister get reconnected, after a long period of separation. That was probably one of the better and more important things I ever did in my life, but it was nothing I dreamed of doing, and nothing you would ever read about in the paper. I still cherish the picture of all of us together that day: my parents, my sister, her kids and grandkids, and me—everyone clear-headed, healthy and happy. This was as it should be, and how it will be, I pray, in heaven.

When I came for that visit to Port Angeles, I stopped to see the Turners as well, and Mrs. Turner (I call her Norma now) said, "You're wise to come when times are good. Often it's only the funeral that brings people together." And she was right, for trouble has never been far from my family of origin. The most painful thing in my life has been seeing how war has continued to wound, even into the third generation after Dad was in it.

Now I'm fifty-eight. I try to be a good husband and father and neighbor, being helpful where I can, and sharing when I can what has most helped me, which is faith. Through my work I support parishes in becoming places where people can truly find God. In my writing I point to God's love and mercy. But the saving part I leave to Christ. It's his job, not mine. Have you ever noticed that Jesus was born on the road, and took to it as a man? He doesn't have to be there. I figure he's out looking for stragglers. He wants no one to be lost (2 *Peter* 3:9).

I said in the prologue that this is a coming-of-age story, but when is one truly grown up? If the measure is being mature in the way I hope to be—selflessly serving God and neighbor—I know I am still miles away from my destination. Seeing how I guard my privileges and comfortable situation, I can only hope that I will be mature by the standard of Christ by the time I die.

But in a lesser way, I do feel grown up. In retrospect, that day in Port Angeles marked my passage into adulthood. Finally I had a clear sense of who I was, where I'd come from, and what had driven me—and I accepted all of that for what it was. If in earlier days I'd been angry with my parents without even realizing it (for how could I be angry with them, knowing they loved me and did their best?), now I was aware of my anger and knew that it was understandable. Their struggles had made me feel I had to fix all our problems, and no child should have to feel that. I saw clearly, too, how the drama of Dad's PTSD kept him 24/7 center-stage in our family, pushing Mom to the periphery, and making her nearly invisible as I looked back.

Today I am deeply grateful to both of them. To Mom for providing for us and standing by Dad, which enabled me to know him as the wise and loving man that he is. And to Dad for speaking up for "the little man" and showing me that God really is always there for you, regardless of what happens.

I started this story with the question "Who cares?" Over time I have had my answer: God does, and countless others do. I rejoice as I recall the many family members, friends, teachers, priests, psychologists, and others who have helped me along the way. God bless them! I have loved writing about them here. Now when I think of those wondrous morning bus rides through the corn fields of Indiana I see the faces of those who were up early to make sure I could learn. I see my mom taking out the juice and pouring the cereal. I see my dad dreaming of a new chance. I see Alice warming up the bus, Mr. Ross cleaning the school, and Mrs. Sutter, Mrs. Brown, and Dr. Bryan all at their desks preparing their lessons.

Now I know the road isn't as lonesome as I thought it was.

Acknowledgments

It took me twenty years to write this book. I thought it would be easy. What could be easier than telling your own story? But try it sometime! First there's the story. What actually *is* the story? Which memories are proper to the story and which are not? Then there are the memories themselves. They prove wobbly, or missing altogether. And then you realize that your own story overlaps with other people's stories, people who may want nothing to do with your memoir.

Throughout the writing I worried I was violating the commandment to honor thy father and thy mother, by airing dirty laundry. But how finally does one best honor thy father and thy mother? What I've learned from Mom and Dad's words and example is that you should tell the truth, have the courage of your convictions, and do what you do out of love. In that spirit I have written this, and now I share it. Countless times in my life I've been helped by writers who dared say how things really were, without shame or apology. I hope I will help someone too.

In the late stage of writing, Mom, Dad, and Tracey shared memories of their own that enabled me to fill in blanks and say things more accurately. I am deeply grateful to them for their understanding, cooperation, and acceptance of my need to publish this. Even more, I am thankful they have continued to struggle along with me in this life to do the right thing and to face down the terrors that be.

Gene and Norma Turner and their daughter, Suzanne (Turner) Shaw, have from the beginning respected and supported my wish to write this book. Sung Yang is another who, like my own family and the Turners, has been present both within the confines of the story and, to this very day, within the larger context of my life. Because of them I've known much joy along the way. Thank you to all of these friends!

Many others helped me produce this book as well. First and foremost, my wife Janke, who read every draft and always pointed out where I was holding back. More fundamentally, she understood my need to commit countless hours to this project, and she shared her own love and wisdom with me. I hope this book gives to her and our children, Annegien and Pieter, lasting value in return for the hours of my attention the writing process deprived them of.

Beyond the abovementioned people, I am also indebted to the following (in alphabetical order) who at some point read and gave feedback on what I'd written: Kevin Cooley, Matthew Cooley, Stijn Fens, Leo Fijen, Julie Fissinger, Jim Forest, Gien de Groot, Klaas de Groot, Jim Hepworth, Fr. Robert Imbelli, Marjet de Jong, Fr. Tom Krieg, John N. Maclean, Nicole Montagne, Fr. Terry Moran, Melanie Morey, Lisa Morrison, Phil Phillips, Bernie Purcell, Mirjam Spruit, Alan Weltzien, and Heidi Wills. Due to their contributions this is a much better book than it would have been otherwise.

Wipf and Stock publishing house helps little-known writers like me to make their books available. I am grateful for their interest in and support in publishing this work. I'm also grateful to *Commonweal* for permission to reprint the text that serves as this book's prologue.

T.P.S.

www.ingramcontent.com/pod-product-compliance
Lightning Source LLC
Chambersburg PA
CBHW051725090426
42738CB00010B/2083